The Singing Assembly

PASTORAL MUSIC IN PRACTICE
6

The Singing Assembly

Edited by Virgil C. Funk

The Pastoral Press
Washington, D.C.

ISBN: 0-912405-80-5

The Pastoral Press
225 Sheridan Street, NW
Washington, D.C. 20011
(202) 723-1254

The Pastoral Press is the publications division of the National
Association of Pastoral Musicians, a membership organization of
musicians and clergy dedicated to fostering the art of musical
liturgy.

Printed in the United States of America

CONTENTS

INTRODUCTION

Surely the two most quoted passages from Vatican II's Constitution on the Sacred Liturgy must be: "The church earnestly desires that all the faithful be led to that full, conscious, and active participation in liturgical celebrations called for by the very nature of the liturgy . . . In the reform and promotion of the liturgy, this full and active participation by all the people is the aim to be considered before all else" (no.14).

The people who gather for the church's ritual prayer do so in response to God's invitation. They are known as the "assembly," namely, the *ekklesia*, the church, those coming together in response to a divine summons. The needs of this assembly were at the very center of all the liturgical reforms initiated by the council: the change to the vernacular, the simplification of rites, the development of a three-year cycle of readings for Mass, the incorporation of a liturgy of the word in every sacramental celebration, and the like. We have moved, and are still continuing to do so, from a priest-centered liturgy to a people-centered liturgy. It is no accident that the very first words of The Order of Mass (in the original Latin) are: *Populo congregato . . .*" ("After the people have assembled . . .").

Part of this shift of focus to the people has been a focus on the song of the people. The prayer of the assembly is primarily sung prayer since singing deepens, expresses, unifies, and vitalizes common prayer. Singing is no esthetic shell for the assembly's prayer together; rather, it is the modality of prayer, the means through which common prayer can best happen. This was well known to the early Christians. St. Augustine writes that apart from the time when the Scriptures are being proclaimed, during the homily, while the bishop is praying aloud, and while the

deacon is announcing the intentions during the general intercessions, "is there any time when the faithful assembled in the
church are not singing? Truly I see nothing better, more useful
or more holy that they could do." (*Ep.* 55:18-19)

Singing assemblies do not just happen. Shared values are as
important as parish leadership and appropriate repertoire. And
yet it is the pastoral musician who plays a crucial role in enabling
the song of the assembly. This volume, composed of selected
articles from past issues of *Pastoral Music*, is designed to help the
musician in this task. The authors treat both theory and practice.
Although their approaches may differ, they share a common
goal, one admirably expressed by Charles Gardner in Chapter
XIV, that pastoral musicians "love the sound of a singing congregation above any other musical sound."

Virgil C. Funk

THE ASSEMBLY AND ITS SONG

ONE

ASSEMBLY: REMEMBERING INTO THE FUTURE

To remember is to become aware of time's mystery and grace's history. It is to become aware that, as human beings and as Christians, our sense of the present is defined by the past that lies behind and the future that calls for decision. To remember into the future is to be aware that our options for the future are always circumscribed by the givenness of the present to which the present has delivered us. It is to be aware that the path we choose for the future, to the degree that we choose it, will be conditioned by our experiences of the past. What has been prompts us to wonder what might yet be. What has happened must make us examine what we have actually achieved. Our experience of past events beyond our control must make us wonder what events, unforeseen and unplanned, await us in the future.

Vatican II was an event which few, if any, of us had any control over, or even foresaw. Over twenty-five years later, while time continues to carry us forward and away from it, still it looms large in the landscape behind us and still we walk in its light. The questions are many. How far have we come? What, in the meantime, has actually happened to us, individually and collectively? What have we learned in the intervening years? What drama have we been playing out upon the world stage, which future historians will identify and say—as we can never say—"Such and such was the meaning of those years; that is what was going on"?

We must all hear and ponder these questions. But my task is to place these questions in a broader context by reflecting on three things. First, what it means to remember. Second, what it means to remember in the liturgical assembly. Third, what remembering into the future might demand of us now, as we approach the end of the twentieth century.

REMEMBERING AND THE FUTURE

In 1974 two psychologists by the names of Thomas Cottle and Stephen Klineberg published a fascinating book entitled *The Present of Things Future: Explorations of Time in Human Experience*. The heart of this study consisted of a series of taped interviews with very ordinary people, designed to discover how they remembered the past, how they saw the future, and what the connection was. They found that people's sense of the future was entirely conditioned by their sense of the past. Those who had a strong sense of continuity in their past life invariably had a strong belief that the future would develop continuously out of the present. Others, whose past seemed to them a series of disconnected happenings over which they had little control, had hopes for the future, but that future seemed totally disconnected from the present and they themselves were taking no steps to bring it about. They were simply waiting for something to turn up, for God or luck to intervene and miraculously transform their lives. And then there were those who found the present difficult to accept: they tended either to live in the past or to dream of the future—anything but live in the present. There were, finally, those in whom the future inspired no confidence: they tended to live entirely in the present—eat, drink, and consume, for tomorrow they may be no tomorrow.

These reflections on memory and anticipation hardly do justice to the book, but they might be enough to help us examine our own sense of the past, present, and future, of where we have come from and where we are going.

In the earliest centuries of the church, while Christ's earthly existence was still a lively historical memory, Christians also had a vivid sense of the future. History, it seemed to them, was rushing to its appointed end, its final consummation in the return of Christ in glory. However, as the past grew more distant, so did the future become vague: the promise of the parousia faded as a memory of Christ's first coming grew more faint. But people cannot live long without a future to look forward to, so the eschatological dimensions of Christian life became foreshortened in two ways. First, the liturgy itself was increasingly understood, not only as pointing to the end but as somehow realizing the end. In the eucharist, the end-time is already present, it was said. The result was to change the direction of the coming kingdom: instead of being a goal at the end of time, it came to be imaged as a world above. The horizontal dimension gave way to the vertical, the spatial model of above and below replaced the temporal model of now and one day soon. At the same time, the temporal dimension did not disappear altogether, but shifted from the history of the race to the history of an individual life: the long-term horizon of the end of the world yielded to the short term horizon of the end of life. With this, the emphasis shifted from the social and historical understanding of Christianity, to a more personal and individualistic one. Instead of the community expecting the end of the world, there was the church preparing people to meet their death. Undoubtedly, this contributed enormously to the rise of indivdualism, for the fate of the earth and the outcome of historical events seemed altogether less urgent than the individual person's more immediate appointment with death and judgment. So the change of historical perspective went hand in hand with the breakdown of the sense of community.

It is all the more striking then that Vatican II, in the liturgy constitution and elsewhere, made a bold attempt to recover both those elements of Christian consciousness: our sense of solidarity with one another, and our sense of responsibility for history as salvation history. It is not at all clear at this stage that our liturgical practice has really captured this memory which Vatican II recovered. We have latched onto the idea of community, but do our liturgies truly reflect this broader understanding of time and history?

It is probably true to say that, in attempting to respond to the church's call for liturgies that are genuine community celebrations, we have largely understood community in psychological terms, as something almost synonymous with "intimacy." As a result, our liturgical assemblies and the music that orchestrates them have sometimes given the impression of being experiments in instant intimacy. The idea of community celebration has been taken up by a culture which is emotionally insecure, committed to instant results, and reliant on techniques to achieve them. But what has happened to our sense of history as God's history, or of our place in that? Is it too much to say that our assemblies, these past twenty-five years, have become introverted, focused on "meaningful worship experiences" and emotional satisfaction, rather than extroverted and dedicated to the accomplishment of God's plan for the world? Certainly the Christian life should have its personal satisfactions, but in the perspective of history, where the church appears as a sociologically identifiable group playing a role in the life and culture of our times, called by God from among the peoples for the accomplishment of his will, such pre-occupation with ourselves and our feelings must appear trivial, if not positively narcissistic.

And there is another curious dimension to this, connected more closely with our failure to recover the sense of history which Vatican II proposed to us. While Vatican II was largely a recovery of our forgotten tradition, and the liturgical reforms were based almost exclusively upon historical research, our liturgical celebrations have been almost entirely stripped of any sense of time. It is as if, in the past two decades, we have been more concerned to forget than to remember. This would be true of our musical heritage, but it is true in even more important ways. For example, so-called traditionalist Catholics who resent the changes often do so because they seem so trivial, so lacking in seriousness. Such a charge is not easily dismissed. The "old liturgy," for all its timelessness, was celebrated with a strong sense of past and future, even if that past tended to dwell somewhat one-sidedly upon the sacrifice of Christ on Calvary and the future was seen almost exclusively in terms of death, judgment, heaven, and hell. But the new liturgy seems even more timeless, in the sense that it focuses, typically, on the here and now: death is but rarely mentioned; prayers for the deceased are for the most part neglected; and the memory of Christ's saving works in the past has given way to a somewhat vague affirmation of his presence in each one of us and in our lives.

In terms of Cottle and Klineberg's analysis, it is almost as if we were people bereft of a past and with no thought for the future. It is as if we wanted to blot out any feelings about past or future. Instant community, spontaneous celebration, disposable music are the order of the day. The call to "remember into the future" is a Christian imperative. It is more than an invitation to reminisce about the last twenty-five years; it is a call to become a community by becoming a people with a memory and a people with a sense of destiny.

ASSEMBLY

Perhaps I can substantiate these reflections by turning more specifically to the matter of the liturgical assembly and how our understanding of it has developed over the past years.

We should begin, I suggest, by remembering the way we were in 1963. There were parishes here and there, of course, which, with visionary leadership, had begun to anticipate the direction in which the council would point us; but, by and large, the American Catholic parishes of the early 1960s were much as they had been for the past 150 years. The churches were full. Mass and the sacraments were in Latin, mumbled through by priest and server before a passive congregation. Catholics were loyal, traditional, and cut off in many ways from the wider society, though Kennedy's accession to the presidency and the universal popularity of John XXIII were finally granting that admission to the mainstream of American life and culture to which Catholics had so long aspired.

With the council, the congregation came to life. The blessed mutter of the Mass before a sniffling, shuffling, kneeling assembly was swept away by a tide of noisy conversation, guitar-strumming, and handclapping. The traditional air of part-boredom, part-recollection yielded to the new gregariousness, the novelty of English texts, and the easy informality of the "new liturgy." The old church seemed to have recovered its youth: "Brothers, sisters, we are one / and our life has just begun" . . . or so it seemed.

The main agenda of those years was less that of remembering into the future than that of breaking with the past and forgetting it. If, at Vatican II, the church regained something of its youth, those postconciliar years now appear to have about them something of the air of adolescence: a certain awkwardness, a gaucherie, an enthusiasm for the new coupled with a certain mistrust of older wisdom, confidence in a brave new future, a repudiation of parental authority, and a clinging to one's peer group. We have aged since then. Kennedy's assassination was the first shock to be rapidly followed by other assassinations, the turbulent years of war in Vietnam and violent protest at home, the scandals of Watergate, the short, sharp horrors associated with names like Jonestown, and the unending agonies of Ulster and Cambodia and Biafra and Iran. And in the church, lesser setbacks, but widespread disenchantment: death of God theology, *Humanae Vitae,* the exodus of so many leaders and potential leaders from the priesthood, from religious life, and even from the church. Yes, we have aged. We have grown for the most part more sober, perhaps more wise; though there are still those who appear unwilling to let go the golden days of the early sixties.

Yet it seems to me that in the mainstream of American Catholicism, between those who will not let go of the preconciliar church and those who will not let go of the postconciliar church, there is a movement into the future which is based on a more profound kind of remembering. Finding the promise of instant community to be illusory and the diet of "meaningful worship experiences" not to be sustaining, we are beginning to engage in the kind of remembering that is perhaps best identified as recollection. It is as if, in the first phase of liturgical renewal, we put ourselves into the center of the liturgy, focusing our activity and attention on ourselves and on one another, compensating, perhaps, for having been kept to the periphery for so long, so long reduced to the role of passive spectators. Now, in the second phase of renewal, there is evidence that we are becoming more reflective. We are remembering again who we are at the liturgy and what it is we are about there. We are beginning to acknowledge the truth of the accusation that we often trivialized something that is essentially serious: not always sombre and grave, but always and necessarily serious. We are remembering that, when we come together, we are no mere bunch of pals, but the living sacrament of the body of the Crucified and Risen Lord. Remembering becomes recollection:

> You have come to Mount Zion
> and to the city of the living God,
> the heavenly Jerusalem,
> and to innumerable angels in festal gathering,
> and to the assembly of the first-born
> who are enrolled in heaven
> and to a judge who is God of all
> and to the spirits of the just made perfect,
> and to Jesus, the mediator of a new covenant,
> and to the sprinkled blood
> that speaks more graciously than the blood of Abel.
>   (Heb 12:22-24)

Perhaps I am being overly optimistic, but it does seem as if, after overcoming our initial reactions to the "old liturgy," we are gradually coming to a more profound appreciation of the objective mystery we encounter in the assembly and its liturgy. One of the favorite patristic quotations of the postconciliar church has half a line from Irenaeus: "The glory of God is humanity fully alive." We stitched it onto our liturgical banners and made it an excuse for all sorts of fun . . . but we forgot the rest of the sentence: "The glory of God is humanity fully alive, but the life of humanity consists in the vision of God." There is a hunger now for the vision of God, a hunger which prompts us to reconsider the objective character of liturgical assembly and celebration: the efficacious and operative presence of the Crucified Lord and of his transforming Spirit.

In coming to such awareness we are beginning to appropriate and apply what theologians have seen as the heart of the liturgy: *remembering*—indeed, remembering into the future. On the basis of studies on the biblical meaning of remembering and memorial, it is clear that the essential activity of the liturgical assembly is that of remembering God in Christ. In the biblical sense, remembering means not only calling the past to mind, but making it the basis of present and future action. To remember the ways of God, for example, is to submit to them; to forget the ways of God is to sin. But such is the relationship between God and the covenant people that, when the people of God gather to remember God and God's saving acts, God "remembers" and acts towards us now with the same saving purpose with which he acted towards his people in the past. To remember is to act. For that reason, too, the psalmist and the church pray God not to remember our sins (which would be to punish us) but to remember the promises of old and the mercy he has shown in the past.

The Christian liturgy is what the Christian assembly does when it gathers: it remembers Christ. This remembering or anamnesis is no mere imaginative recall, however. To remember Christ is to identify with Christ in his submission to God, to identify with his sacrifice and self-surrender in order to become, like Christ, the objects of God's saving remembrance. "Father, calling to mind the death your Son endured for our salvation, his glorious resurrection and ascension into heaven, and ready to greet him when he comes again, we offer you in thanksgiving this holy and living sacrifice." Such is the burden of every eucharistic prayer. And "this holy and living sacrifice" which we offer is the Body of Christ, surrendered in sacrifice, which St. Augustine does not hesitate to describe as "your own mystery": "When the priest says, 'The Body of Christ' and you say 'Amen,' you say 'Amen' to your own mystery." The assembly, remembering Christ in a profound act of recollection, discovers its own mystery, its identity as the Body of Christ in the world, continuing to surrender to God and to the work of God, until the end of time, ("ready to greet him when he comes again"). The liturgy itself is essentially an act of remembering into the future, in which we submit ourselves again and again to the plan of God for human history and commit ourselves to its realization. The eucharist recollects our past and shapes our future.

If this brief sketch of a theology of remembering in the liturgy makes any sense, it is clear that the way the liturgy is celebrated needs to foster the mood of profound recollection, that we might come to awareness of "Christ among us, our hope of glory." We come to the liturgy not so much to express ourselves as to find ourselves; not to vocalize the faith we already feel but to be drawn into the faith and fidelity of Christ himself; not to create a sense of community but to discover the unimaginable mystery of our common life in Christ and in his Spirit; not to be instructed by songs and sermons but to open ourselves to the instruction of the Spirit. The liturgy is indeed less concerned with what we know ourselves to be, than with bringing us to discover who we really are.

This has many implications for liturgical music—or better, for sung prayer. We need music which will help us remember who we are and in whose presence we stand; and I believe such music is gradually becoming available once again. It is music which is neither background nor accompaniment to prayer, still less a mere community-forming device in preparation for prayer. It is music which lends itself to prayerful remembrance of things past, present, and future, which lends itself to contemplative recollection. It is music which avoids the temptation to be didactic or to express moods and feelings which may or may not be those of the assembled faithful. It is music which knows its place, attaching itself to certain parts of the liturgy rather than others, and to certain times of the liturgical year. It is music which not only bears repetition, but requires it, for repetition is the mother of memory, both in ritual and in music. Liturgical music, like liturgical ritual, is esssentially repeatable, because it is only by being sung over and over again at appropriate moments that it can work upon our forgetfulness and bring us to realize the mystery we are engaged in. Liturgical music, like the liturgy as a whole, cannot work its full effect in a single celebration. It works on us over the years, over a lifetime, over the centuries, as an instrument of the Spirit in the church, bringing to our realization all that Christ has given us and leading the church, contemplatively, into the fullness of truth.

THE FUTURE INTO WHICH WE REMEMBER

This last mention of the long-term effects of the liturgy, as the activity of the assembled church, remembering, leads naturally to my final set of reflections, which have to do with the scope of the remembering we ought to engage in.

The theme "remembering into the future" inevitably raises the question of how far back we ought to remember and how far forward we should peer into the future. Our understanding of the present is largely conditioned by how we set our sights. For example, in response to the question of what brought me to the convention at which the ideas in this article were originally expressed, I could mention the flight that landed me in the city where the convention took place, or the period of time that I spent thinking about this paper and working on it. I could also speak of my experiences over the years, of the training I received which prompted the invitiation to address the convention and my acceptance. I could go back even further to events before my birth, to tell the story of people like my father and godfather, whose Catholic experience was so influential in my own formation. And one could go on pushing back to the beginning: for when you begin to remember and to recount, any starting point is necessarily artificial. And the same would be true of the future. The scope of the hoped-for-future can be endlessly enlarged, though, like all enlargements, the picture grows more blurred with each successive enlargement.

I have already suggested that our remembering needs to go further and deeper than the last twenty-five years. We shall be untrue to our times, to our faith, and to the future if Vatican II is the sole extent of our sense of time and history. For generations yet unborn, our time will be remembered, not perhaps as the century of Vatican II, but as the century of great progress and incredible regression, as the century of wars and violence, and of peace through the threat of mutual annihilation. It will be remembered as the century of moon rockets and gas chambers, a century where medicine leapt forward and where people destroyed one another on a scale hitherto undreamt of. It will be remembered as the time of the holocaust and genocide—of the holocaust which shunted ten-thousand people a week to their deaths, and of the holocaust of nuclear destruction which overshadows our future. We are not only a people who celebrated the reformed liturgy: we are, as David Power has said, a people called to celebrate between the holocausts.

When historians of liturgy look back on our celebrations, will they judge us a people who remembered or a people who tried to forget? Where does the terrible liturgy of anguish and death and grace and hope, played out in our history, find any reflection in our prayer, our celebration, or our music? How can we sing "God hears the cries of the poor" to a tripping little melody without the memory of the ovens of Auschwitz and the silence of

God disturbing us? The passover liturgy went forward undisturbed as Christ was crucified on Golgotha, as if the people and priests who recalled the salvation of old were trying to forget their responsibility for the present. They missed the once-for-all sacrifice for the world's salvation. And we, too, run the risk of deluding ourselves about the liturgy and celebrating if we attempt to safeguard our faith by choosing not to remember too much.

So much for the past; yet, the way we relate to the future is largely determined, as we have seen, by what we remember from the past. So often, at the beginning of our liturgy workshops at Notre Dame, participants will say: "Well, in our parish we've done the same thing for the past two years, so we're looking for some new ideas." I suppose many of us have similar thoughts of the future: only let it be different. But this, I suggest, is an exercise in forgetting. We are called to "remember into the future." Although this does not preclude the making of short-term plans, it is essentially an invitation to take stock of where we are and to situate ourselves in the face of a rather longer future.

We are called to look beyond Vatican II's implications for today and tomorrow. Karl Rahner did just that. For him the fundamental theological significance of Vatican II is to be found in the fact that, at the Second Vatican Council, the Catholic Church appeared, for the first time in its nearly two-thousand year history, as a truly world church, rather than a religion of the Mediterranean basin and of Europe. For the first time, he points out, the churches outside Europe and North America were represented, not by missionary bishops, but by their own pastors. For the first time, the Catholic Church had a vision of itself as becoming truly catholic. Of course, he admits, that vision still remains to be fully implemented, but it is something that we cannot easily forget: Catholic Christianity belongs not to European civilization, but to the world.

This transformation of the church he finds to have only one historical parallel—in the transplanting of Christianity from its Judeo-Christian seed-bed into the pagan soil of the Graeco-Roman world. He writes:

> Theologically speaking, there are just three great epochs in Church history, of which the third has just begun and made itself observable officially at Vatican II. First, the short period of Jewish

Christianity. Second, the period of a Church in a distinct cultural region, namely, that of Hellenism and of European culture and civilization. Third, the period in which the sphere of the Church's life is in fact the whole world.[1]

Each of these periods, he points out, provided very different contexts and very different challenges to Christianity and its preaching—and also, we might add, to its liturgical celebration and its musical forms.

What does it do to our self-awareness, to our attempt to remember into the future, when we think of ourselves as living through a profound transformation of Christianity, one as radical and far-reaching as the change from the church being a Jewish sect to being the religion of Europe? What does it do to our sense of responsibility for the future to consider ourselves as standing on the threshold of the third great age of the church? Richard McBrien underlines the question by pointing out that we usually tend to think of the history of the church as long and of the future as short. But what, he asks, if the church should survive to the year 19083?—and there is no theological reason why it should not. To Christians living in that year of grace, we would appear to be members of the early church.

The effect of both these suggestions—the one concerning the theological significance of Vatican II, the other a challenge to our usual way of envisaging our place on the graph of history—is to force us to reconsider the meaning of this moment and to reexamine the responsibilities of our place in history. Very often, when we consider our responsibility for the future, we think no further than our own children and our cherished hope that they will remain true to the faith we know. The result, as we know from our own experience of growing up, is that they are equipped only with a childish faith, inadequate for their future lives. In the light of the vastly enlarged horizons offered by Rahner and McBrien, however, we can see that we have a responsibility, not only to our own children, but to history and to the God of history. The question is not how can we ensure that our children will grow up Catholic like us, but rather, what is the meaning of this tradition we have received, and in what condition shall we pass it on to generations yet unborn? Will there be found faith on the earth in 19083, and what will have been our contribution to its transmission? From that perspective, looking back, will our liturgy be judged a liturgy of faith or of delusion, of remembering or of forgetting, of serious confrontation with the reality of historical existence or mere escapism?

Rahner's perspective is particularly challenging for, if he is right, the changes we are involved in are likely to be far more profound and far-reaching than any of us supposed. It is not merely a matter of trading postconciliar for preconciliar styles. If our tradition is destined to undergo as radical a transformation in the move from being European to being truly catholic as it did in developing from a Jewish sect into the religion of the Graeco-Roman world, then we are going to have to have a much more profound grasp of what is truly foundational in our faith and practice. Our remembering of the mysteries handed down to us will require us to move beyond our preoccupation with fads and trivialities, beyond the incessant search for decorative novelties which occupy so much of our attention and engage so much of our energies.

Fortunately, this second transformation, like the first, will find theology chasing to catch up with change rather than dictating its pattern. This means that we should devote our attention, not to inventing new forms which may or may not last, but to remembering the deep things of faith. Better to devote ourselves to the tasks of recollection, for it is the memory of the church as a whole and the guidance of the Spirit which will enable us to remember into the future. Ultimately, as we have learned from the liturgy, it is Christ who remembers, who is remembered, and who is looked for in the future. "He is alpha and omega; all times belong to him and all the ages." He stands in our past; he images our future; he redeems our present. To him be glory, through the Holy Spirit in the holy church, now and always and unto ages of ages. Amen.

Note

1. Karl Rahner, "Towards a Fundamental Theological Interpretation of Vatican II," *Theological Studies* 40 (1979) 721.

John Gurrieri

TWO

FULL, CONSCIOUS, AND ACTIVE PARTICIPATION IS FOR ALL THE FAITHFUL

The evolution of Christian thought and activity since Vatican II is matched by few other periods in the long history of the church. Our era, despite what some commentators say, is a hopeful one. The great dogmatic and pastoral constitutions that issued from Vatican II, the largest assemblage of bishops in the history of the church, challenge Christians in our own time and for generations to come. Our agenda is weighty indeed, with questions of Christian unity, liturgical and spiritual renewal, and, most fundamentally, a new understanding and appreciation of the church: its role in the world and its nature as an institution. The renewal of ecclesiology is perhaps the most important long-range result of the council. The relationship between particular communities and the "church universal" has found expression in new ecclesial institutions and ministries such as the episcopal conference, the diocesan pastoral council, the senate or council of priests, and the parish council. These indicate a new level of participation—by *all the baptized*—in the structured authority of the church and in their Christian birthright.

This right is affirmed in *Lumen Gentium* (art. 9), the dogmatic constitution on the church:

> ... those who believe in Christ, who are reborn not from a perishable but from an imperishable seed through the Word of the living God, not from the flesh but from water and the Holy Spirit, are finally established as a "chosen race, a royal priesthood, a holy

17

nation, a purchased people . . . You who in times past were not a people, but are now the people of God" . . . The heritage of this people are the dignity and freedom of the [children] of God, in whose hearts the Holy Spirit dwells as in His temple.

So the dignity and freedom of the people of God have gained recognition, and the people of God, according to the council, comprises all members of the church, not just the laity but the ordained as well. Compare this attitude to the following sentiment, as stated in 1839 but probably familiar to many:

Now, by what means are the laity instrumental in the performance of this great and good work [the propagation of the faith]? Have they been commissioned, like the Apostles, to preach the gospel of peace? Have they received that exalted character, by which they are to be recognized as "ministers of Christ and the dispensers of the mysteries of God"? No; their station is of a subordinate kind; but however inferior in point of dignity to the rank of the Apostles, it imposes duties which, if uniformly practiced, must exert a most happy influence upon a society at large, and vastly contribute to the dissemination of the true faith.[1]

We have come a long way. In the old view, not only were roles distinct, but people were subordinated to some "greater dignity" belonging to a few. This was a practical theology, taking its cue not from Scripture or tradition but from a socio-political ideology in which privilege dominated and government did not concern itself with the common good. This ecclesiology found expression in Christian worship: the people assisted at the function of the liturgy, joining themselves through *pia exercitia* to the sacrifice offered God by the church's priest; but the rites, symbols, and even the architecture of the liturgy underscore the sense that the ordained were somehow in opposition to the unordained. It was as if the unordained were somehow abnormal or at best somewhat short of fully possessing the grace of Christ. Being faithful meant being subordinate or obedient.

The ecclesiology most often enunciated by popes, bishops, and theologians before Vatican II emphasized hierarchy and authority. Pope Pius X, who had written of the "right and duty" of Christians as a royal people and a holy nation to participate in the liturgy, also maintained in his *Vehementer Nos*:

In the hierarchy alone reside the power and authority necessary to move and direct all the members of society to its end. As for the many, they have no other right than to let themselves be guided and so follow their pastors in docility.

The most harmful product of this historical development was the barrier between clergy and laity, not merely on the basis of day-to-day life in the church, but also in the realm of speculative theology. And the single most important question that is up for reassessment is what it means to be one of the "faithful," a member of the praising assembly of God's people.

THE FAITHFUL AND PARTICIPATION

To many, the "faithful" are the lay men and women of the church. This lopsided conception is found even in the documents of Vatican II, in which the use of the word is often ambiguous. Nevertheless, a distinct viewpoint emerges that the laity are part of the whole people of God, *all* of whom are the "faithful." It is true that here and there in the documents, less accurate uses can be found, such as "pastors and the faithful" or "priests and the faithful," but the more authentic meaning of the word was indeed recaptured by the council.

First of all, the very word itself, "faithful," is a technical word (in Latin, *fidelis*) that belongs to the terminology of Christian initiation. A *fidelis* is someone who has received the greatest gift from God—faith—which comes only with and at the moment of baptism, not before. In the newly restored rites of initiation, as in the ancient process, "faithful" is equivalent to "communicant"— one who is not only baptized and confirmed (anointed), but also in communion with Christ and other Christians through full participation in the eucharist. Eucharistic communion is the highest expression of Christian fellowship and faith. And since only the faithful can be present for and participate in the eucharistic mystery, the word serves better to distinguish the fully initiated from inquirers and catechumens than it does to distinguish laity from clergy.

Thus, the context for understanding this often misunderstood word is *participation* in the eucharist and *not* status within the

community of believers by reference to ordination. All the faithful participate in the one priesthood of Jesus Christ, and ordination is the church's constitutive response to the corresponding
need for eucharist and therefore for that church order imaged in
the eucharist.

Pius X, despite other aspects of his ecclesiology, did establish
that the "right and duty" of all the "faithful" to full participation
in the liturgy was primordial to liturgical renewal in the church.
Pius XII, in the encyclical *Mystici Corporis*, developed this stance
under the influences of the great theologians of the 1930s and
1940s. The liturgical movement in America and abroad agitated
for ritual reforms that would actualize what was then only a
theory. All these strands eventually went into the fabric of the
historic Constitution on the Sacred Liturgy, the first document
promulgated by the council, which made total liturgical reform
the first priority of the church. The magnificent statement of
principle for this goal is contained in number 14 of the constitution:

> Mother Church earnestly desires that all the faithful be led to that
> full, conscious, and active participation in liturgical celebrations
> which is demanded by the very nature of the liturgy. Such par-
> ticipation by the Christian people as "a chosen race, a royal priest-
> hood, a holy nation, a purchased people (1 Pet 2:9; cfr. 2:4-5), is
> their right and duty by reason of their baptism.
>
> In the restoration and promotion of the sacred liturgy, this full and
> active participation by all the people is the aim to be considered
> before all else; for it is the primary and indispensable source from
> which the faithful are to derive the true Christian spirit. Therefore,
> through the needed program of instruction, pastors of souls must
> zealously strive to achieve it in all their pastoral work.

We have perhaps grown too accustomed to the principle that
"full, conscious, and active participation . . . is demanded by the
very nature of the liturgy," and even begun to take it lightly. And
perhaps we haven't fully considered the point that "the faithful
. . . derive the true Christian spirit" through participation. In
other words, the worship experience, especially the celebration of
the eucharist, is the source and foundation of Christian existence.
The lessons to be learned from "full, conscious, and active par-

ticipation" in the liturgy are lessons that Christians must apply to the whole spectrum of Christian life.

So if in 1839 one could speak only of a "subordinate" participation in the church's mission for the laity, this was simply mirroring the role of lay people in worship at that time. If Pius X emphasized the docility of the laity, it was because passivity was the only possible response to an overly hierarchical liturgy.

The church has yet to achieve the goals it set for itself at Vatican II. The years between the Council of Trent and the Second Vatican Council were spent consolidating the Tridentine reforms in the crucible of experience, debate, and even polemic. This period (1564-1963), however, was not the monolith that reactionary conservatives today seem to think it was. Even in the late nineteenth century, there were still towns and villages in various corners of Europe that would not accept the liturgical reforms of the Council of Trent. By and large, in fact, the great dogmatic statements of the council that were made for the sake of Christian unity were not used to achieve that end; rather, they were used against dissenters and non-Catholics. The evolution of doctrine evident at the Council of Trent was largely ignored by succeeding generations of theologians, who saw the Tridentine decrees as items for exegesis rather than as fodder for theological reflection. The impetus for evangelization and catechesis projected by Trent was certainly evident in the birth of new religious orders; but the evangelization of the millions in Asia and the Americas most often resembled the mass conversions of the Constantinian era rather than the preaching and baptizing of the apostolic church or the catechumenate of patristic times. In short, there is a lesson to be learned in our own time. We now have the choice between paying lip service to the great work of Vatican II and seizing the opportunity to discover the many implications of the conciliar challenge.

THE TASK AT HAND

First of all, we must learn the significance of fidelity to the Lord Jesus and his Gospel. Perhaps we must begin with the lesson of human fidelity. Do we truly understand what it means to be faithful to a friend, spouse, parent, associate, or even "authority"? It is easy to lament our age as a faithless one, a time in which people do not care about one another. And there are signs of infidelity all around us. Yet the radical truth of our humanity is the desire not to be alone but to know and ultimately to love and be loved by others.

To be one of the "faithful" of the church is all that human fidelity signifies and quite a bit more. Our initiation into the mystery of Christ has given us the ability, the "grace favor," to recognize something that is hidden in our humanity. We need to wake up to the fact, as Karl Rahner says, "that the detailed events and actions of concrete human existence are always in fact, even in their naturalness, something more than merely natural." Rahner gives this example:

> When . . . a concrete human being . . . experiences genuine personal love for another human being, it always has a validity, an eternal significance and an inexpressible depth which it would not have had but that such a love is so constituted as to be a way of actualizing the love of God as a human activity springing from God's own act.[2]

The reason for this actualization of God's own love in our loving is the fidelity of Christ Jesus who died and rose from the dead for all men and women. Christ's action has altered the course of human existence. And that action, the mystery of his death and resurrection, has enabled anyone who enters into the mutual covenant of fidelity with God through baptism both to recognize God's action within human action, and ultimately, to enter into the very life of God. Christian initiation brings us to another realm and another dimension of perception, where we discover both the significance of the individual whom God calls by name and the need for the community as people who love and are loved to mirror the love of the Trinity. Again, as Karl Rahner states: "When God loves, his love is truly creative. It fully and really makes what is loved into what it is loved as."[3]

To be one of the "faithful" implies both the growth of the individual and the discovery of one's self as a necessary part of the community. There is no opposition of one individual to another, for all are baptized. If there is a difference, it is because some, through ordination, are given the mandate within church order to serve and preside for the sake of fidelity.

The second implication of the renewal of the church, and especially the renewal of worship, is that the reformed eucharist, while it is not perfect and does not fulfill all our expectations, enables us better to know who we are as Christians. The Order of Mass, for example, is structured around the assembly as the primary sign of the eucharist. By contrast, the former Order of Mass, in the Missal of Pius V (1570), gave rubrics for everyone involved in the celebration *except the assembly*. The Mass was celebrated *for* the people rather than *by* the people. The Introduction preceding the Mass texts in the old missal not only favored an extremely hierarchical theology of eucharist and church, but it also expressed a theology of grace, which asserts that the Mass is the highest form of piety—that the greatest number of graces is attached to the Mass.

In short, the previous missal as a book in use by the church presented a slightly distorted notion of grace. The absence of a role for the assembly made this most clear, and perpetuated an unfortunate, but completely integrated, ecclesiological world view of liturgy, church institutions, hierarchical ministry, and the role of the laity—all along the lines of Pius X's encyclical. Those who wish a return to the "old Mass" are not merely nostalgic for Latin and the piety of their childhood; they miss the ecclesiology that was superseded by *Lumen Gentium* and *Sacrosanctum Concilium*, by which to be "faithful" meant being one of the laity, and therefore subordinate and docile to the clergy in all matters, even action in the world.

The eucharist that we celebrate today as a praising assembly rejects this world view and its parallels in the speculative and practical theologies of the church. The structure of the eucharist and the ministries it calls forth clarify the nature of the church and the role fulfilled by all the baptized in the world and in the life of the church. No longer is the assembly passively attentive, "assisting" at Mass. No longer does the priest fulfill every ministerial function from presider to reader to congregation. Now all have specific functions to carry out, as the General Instruction of the Roman Missal so clearly spells out: "Everyone in the eucharistic assembly has the right and duty to take his own part according to the diversity of orders and functions" (no. 58). The functions, and the manner in which they are carried out, mirror the relationship of each of the baptized in all ecclesial matters, not just liturgical ones.

We have finally achieved the ultimate distinction between the old and the new ecclesiologies: we have moved from the *sacerdos celebrans* to the *populus celebrans*. The priest is a celebrant (not *the* celebrant) within the celebrating assembly. He does preside over their worship, but he does not celebrate for them. The praising assembly, made up of all the faithful, the *congregatio fidelium* of Thomas Aquinas, is the image of the church and the principle by which the church must now operate and live.

Notes

1. *The Metropolitan Catholic Almanace and Laity's Directory for the Year of Our Lord 1839*, p.3.
2. Karl Rahner, *The Christian Commitment: Essays in Pastoral Theology* (New York: Herder and Herder, 1963) 51.
3. Ibid. 84.

THREE

THE ART OF ASSEMBLY-ING

Different styles of liturgy are needed for different groups. This truism is easy to state, but it is much harder to decide how to apply the principle concretely. How is it that a liturgy can be carefully planned and executed, and yet one gets the feeling that the celebration has not "clicked"? In this article I will suggest how different models of the church call for different styles of liturgical celebration.

Almost everyone who does church-related work has heard of Avery Dulles' book *Models of the Church*, which proposed five different models or ways of "imaging" the church: as institution, as community, as sacrament, as herald of the word, and as servant. These were refreshing ideas that put names to new experiences of church, coming after centuries when the institutional model predominated so exclusively.

MICRO AND MACRO CHURCH

All of Dulles' models, however, presuppose a highly developed and structured church community. We know that this is not how it all began. The building block of the early church was the little house church. This basic unit has been called the *ecclesiola*, the Latin diminutive of *ecclesia*. The early church was made up of small groups of people who knew one another quite closely. They met for prayer, for fellowship, and for the breaking of the bread. In the course of time these little house churches began to connect with one another, to celebrate their faith in larger assemblies, and to collaborate on a larger scale in looking after their common needs. And so there emerged what we now call the *ecclesia*.

The names I will use for these two models of the church are *micro church* and *macro church*. The micro church is the *ecclesiola*, the household church, which is characterized by intimacy, a strong sense of fellowship, and little formal organization. The macro church is the *ecclesia*, an assembly of little house churches, which is characterized by an organized creed and cult and, inevitably, by greater anonymity.

Both these realities are as recognizable today as they were in the second century. The macro church for most people today is the parish, a gathering of many families and smaller communities. This assembly of household churches is visibly incarnated in the Sunday assembly. The *ecclesiola* or micro church is the small group, a unit of the parish that gathers because of a special interest. This is the "house church" of the New Testament era, a unit based on close fellowship and the experience of intimacy. In every age people have felt the need for such groups, which are the "basic Christian communities" out of which the *ecclesia* is built.

In the past we had the Holy Name Society and the Altar Society. Today people find the experience of micro church in Cursillo, or Marriage Encounter, or Renew groups, or lay ministry groups of all kinds. Many musicians find the experience of micro church in their choirs and scholas and groups dedicated to the ministry of music. For many people, happily, the family is still the most basic Christian community.

These two forms of church are complementary. Each needs the other, and they always exist in a state of creative tension.

Without the macro church, micro churches are likely to become inbred, focused only on their own interests, lacking a breadth and sense of largeness. All of us have had the experience of small groups that served their purpose for a time, but then disbanded or evolved into something else. The virtue of micro-church groups is that they have a fluidity and flexibility about them, a loose and informal organizational structure. This lack of structure is precisely what enabled these units to focus their attention on close fellowship and intimacy.

At the same time, the macro church is not effective without micro churches. The macro church, such as a parish, which is not fed by the life of micro churches in its midst is likely to become clerical, sterile, and impersonal. Like any large institution, the macro church has a tendency to become preoccupied with the abstract good of the whole and to forget the needs of real people. It is no secret that Catholics who cannot find intimacy in their experience of the *ecclesia* go elsewhere to find it, in other churches or in cults that promise fellowship and mutual caring.

The Sunday assembly is always to some extent what someone has called a "company of strangers." The macro church is meant to be an assembly of people who share their faith and experience Christian fellowship in their households and in other small units. When this experience is lacking, we find the situation that is common in so many of our parishes today: instead of being an assembly of household churches, the Sunday gathering becomes that well-known assembly of individuals whom it is so difficult to move out of their private inner spaces.

In your roles as musicians, when you stand up in front of an assembly on Sunday morning, have you ever gotten that sinking feeling that everyone is sitting there quietly saying "Just try to touch me!"? This is the "assembly of individuals," gathered as if for private devotions in a public place. There is no ill will, but we've got a massive liturgical problem before we even begin to deal with the music.

The assembly that remains only a collection of individuals who never become anything more than spectators is a problem that isn't solved by liturgical renewal alone. Creating a liturgical assembly is a function of total parish renewal, which involves the building of small groups and micro churches of all kinds within the parish. Parish renewal begins to happen when micro churches start to come into being.

Rite of Gathering

Ministers of music can begin meeting this problem through an effective use of the rite of gathering. This is a separate unit of the Sunday liturgy, a separate rite from that of the word and the table. It is also the rite that usually needs the most work and gets the least.

The word "liturgy" means the people's action, the assembly's *action*. Each part of the liturgy consists of essential actions: proclaiming our common story, calling for a response, giving thanks, breaking bread and sharing the cup. These actions are the starting points for deciding about the music or any other elements in the liturgy. Although we have come a long way from the four-hymn syndrome, I don't believe that we take enough account of the essential *action* of each part of the service.

Musicians, lectors, and presiders alike tend to be "book people" when they plan liturgies. We have the sacramentary, the lectionary, books of prayers, books of readings, books of songs. We take the approach that this comes here, that goes there. Here is a reading, there's a prayer, and now comes the song. We do all this because "the book says so." What we often don't ask is, what does the book mean? What does the book *intend* for this part of the liturgy?

The essential action of the rite of gathering is to gather and form the faithful into a worshiping assembly. To accomplish this action is not an easy task, especially when you have an assembly of individuals whose only experience of church is the macro church. For musicians, the question is not what opening hymn or Lord Have Mercy or Glory to God to choose. The question is how to use music to gather this group of people together and form them into an assembly that is ready to hear the word of God and break bread together.

What does the book, the sacramentary, offer us for the gathering rite? A real smorgasbord. The book talks about processions, greetings, baptismal blessing and sprinklings with water, penitential petitions with "Lord have mercy," the option of a lengthy hymn proclaiming "Glory to God in the highest," and an opening prayer. What are we to make of all of this, this Sunday, in this parish assembly?

The fact is that our ritual books can't be read correctly unless we read the principles underlying them. Anyone who works with liturgy should read the first chapter of the General Instruction of the Roman Missal, a very short chapter which is found at the beginning of the sacramentary. It states that "each and every liturgy should take into account the nature and circumstances of each assembly." It is therefore "very important to select and arrange the forms and elements proposed" in the sacramentary which will "best foster active and full participation of the faithful" in the liturgy.

"Select and arrange." Key words, which certainly apply to the rite of gathering. Among the forms and elements provided by the ritual, which are the ones that will best accomplish the action that is the essential action of this rite, namely, gathering people together? Music is a powerful tool for gathering, but it will lose much of its power unless the gathering rite is intelligently planned. Too often this part of the Sunday worship becomes a hodge-podge of songs and prayers with no real coherence or focus to it.

TWO BASIC STYLES OF WORSHIP: MACRO-CHURCH LITURGY AND MICRO-CHURCH LITURGY

Let me return to the distinction between micro church and macro church. These models of the church are helpful for naming the two basically different styles of worship. I have said that when it comes to prayer and worship, most Catholics tend to be "book people." There are a lot of good ideas and fine prayers in our liturgical books. But how effective is it to use the same book, the same official liturgy, for both the micro church and the macro church?

Micro-church liturgy is small-group liturgy. It focuses on the needs of a group of people who know one another quite well. This is the place for distinctive cultures to express themselves, whether it be teen-agers or senior citizens, Renewal groups or ethnic groups, your baptismal teams or your CCD teachers. When micro churches like these worship together, their liturgy is likely to focus on the personal, the more intimate. There will be more spontaneously shared prayer, improvised forms, and the music that is sung is likely to have more personal sentiments.

Macro-church liturgy, on the other hand, is by definition *assembly liturgy*. This is the kind of liturgy that our official books were written for—and, I would suggest, the only kind of liturgy where the official books work well.

Over the past few decades, common sense has taught us to be flexible with "the book" when we are celebrating in groups of five or ten people. Have you ever been in a household setting where one of the official eucharistic prayers is proclaimed with five people around the table? It sounds a little strange, a little too solemn, too formal for micro-church worship. Many Catholics today are rediscovering the natural forms of table fellowship. We can break bread and share a cup in Jesus' name with simple prayers of blessing. We can do this even without an ordained minister, just as the first generations of Christians broke bread and shared the cup in their homes.

Many of the forms of assembly liturgy, macro-church liturgy, do not work well in small groups. Conversely, forms of prayer and song that fit well in micro churches do not work in the Sunday assembly.

For example, have you ever been annoyed when the prayer of the faithful is thrown open to personal petitions from the congregation? Your annoyance is legitimate. Often the private petitions can't be heard by the assembly, and too often people will use their petition as a platform for preaching about something. Shared prayer is important in micro-church liturgy, but it doesn't work in the Sunday assembly.

The same is true of much of the music that is usually classified as folk music. Many of the songs recorded by the monks of Weston Priory are excellent for small groups. They have a pleasant and easy melody. The texts of the songs have an intimacy and a personal piety about them that is very powerful in a micro-church group. But just as a small group is not inclined to sing "A Mighty Fortress," neither can we expect many of the Weston Priory's songs to work well in a Sunday assembly. The strength of these songs, which lies in their personal and intimate character, often becomes a liability in assembly liturgy.

To determine what is appropriate for assembly liturgy— whether it be music, ritual action, or forms of prayer—we need to have a clear idea of the purpose of the Sunday liturgy. How is assembly liturgy different from small-group liturgy?

MACRO-CHURCH LITURGY

Assembly focuses on the *ecclesia*, the *catholica*, the Great Church. All of these words are meant to evoke largeness—the largeness of Christ, the universality of his message, the largeness of the communion of saints to which we belong. It is this largeness that is the focus of the Sunday liturgy. The Gospel and the eucharistic prayer proclaim the largeness of God in history and the breadth of the story in which we are called to take part. The liturgy of word and eucharist proclaims the wonders of God that have yet to be achieved in this world, this community, this particular parish.

The intimacy and close fellowship that characterize micro churches need to be complemented by the hope and vision of the *catholica*, without which micro churches will tend to close in on themselves. The Sunday assembly is meant to provide this dimension of largeness and to summon us beyond what already is. Here is the power and uniqueness of macro-church liturgy. When it is done right, it provokes growth in consciousness, it prods our minds and hearts to think and feel larger, more largely than here and now, this place and this time.

When it is done right, the liturgy of the Great Church lets us know and experience that we belong to a past and to a future. Good assembly liturgy lets me experience that my own story belongs to a larger story, and that is the story of Abraham and Moses and Jesus, of Sarah and Esther and Mary the mother of Jesus. And if assembly liturgy is really good, it lets me know that I also belong to Martin Luther and John Calvin, to Martin Luther King and Gandhi and Mother Teresa, and to the people right around me who care for others as Jesus said we should care. Assembly liturgy calls me to celebrate myself and who I am and what I do in *medio ecclesiae*, in the midst of the assembly, where I experience that Christ is in me and I am in Christ.

Good assembly liturgy is not an experience of clerical triumphalism. It is an experience of connectedness with the greatness of God in Christ and in his Body.

Assembly liturgy cannot be planned around the lowest common denominator. When that happens, we get into the pattern of commemorating the past, canonizing the values of our parents' generation, and singing the good old hymns. Many of those hymns are good indeed, and many of our parents' values are excellent. But assembly liturgy has to be something more than what Tammy Baker did on TV.

No one in today's church has an edge on understanding the kind of *experience* of macro church that I have been suggesting here. The average parish priest today spends more time meeting the needs of micro churches than he does in leading and gathering together the macro church, the *ecclesia*. Preparation for the Sunday assembly is not a priority for some pastors, which is most unfortunate and terribly misguided, but one can name some of the reasons why. As the Catholic priesthood has evolved in recent times, the life of the priest has come to revolve around services to micro churches. Apart from the Sunday liturgy itself, the life of most parish priests is filled with private sacramental celebrations: private funerals, private confessions, a dozen private weddings in June, and Masses every day for small groups. We have not yet developed a theology of ministry which sees the presbyter's role as that of gathering the *ecclesia* and fostering the formation of micro churches, rather than providing ritual services to micro churches.

Micro churches have to learn to celebrate by themselves and to lead their own prayer. The leaders of prayer within micro churches are meant to be lay people, not the ordained. Keep in mind that there are no rubrics for small groups, no official books. If we want to get together to pray and break bread and sing a song, we are free to do it. Indeed we are called to do it. When micro churches have taken responsibility for their own life of prayer and ritual, the faithful are likely to develop a stronger and better understanding of what the liturgy of the whole assembly is all about.

We do not yet have the "assembly attitude" that I have been trying to describe. We often prepare assembly liturgy with micro-church models in mind, with songs and forms of prayer which worked so well in a group of twenty people that we want to do them with the assembly too. Macro-church liturgy needs hymnody that uses a more universal language than what a micro church needs. I have suggested how song texts that lean toward private piety and very personal sentiments often don't work well in assembly liturgy. Examples of this are found not just in folk music. Some of the great hymns by Bach or Wesley are attached to texts that are centered on personal piety, and thus are more appropriate for small groups or private prayer. On the other hand, many contemporary compositions composed around biblical texts and the universal language of the Great Church prove to be excellent for assembly liturgy.

The challenge for musicians is to reflect on what assembly liturgy is meant to celebrate. I have proposed the images of the *catholica*, the largeness of Christ and the Gospel, and our connectedness with the past and the future in the communion of saints. These images evoke a form of intimacy and fellowship that is different from micro-church experiences, but deeply in need of good celebration and effective proclamation.

FOUR

DO IT WITH STYLE

A man saw Elbon on his knees, searching for something on the ground. "What have you lost?" he asked.

"My key," said Elbon.

So the man went down on his knees, too, and they both searched for it.

After a time, the other man asked Elbon, "Where exactly did you drop it?"

"In my own house."

"Then why are you looking here?"

"There is more light here than inside my own house."

Traditional Middle Eastern Story

Every worshiping community faces three musical challenges: How to get our asembly to sing, how to sustain our singing, and how to improve our singing. I am a firm believer in the principle that musicians make music and good musicians make good music. And so the first and best way to improve congregational song is by engaging the talents of a good musician.

It is also my belief that sustaining congregational song is a challenging activity, requiring the talents and energy of the musician, the presider, and indeed every member of the assembly in a conscious and deliberate effort to provide song in worship. The adage, "When people have something to sing about, they will sing," is perfectly true.

The first steps to provide congregational song are as follows:

a. Get a good musician,
b. and know that it will take sustained effort
c. by everyone
d. to make sure the congregation has something to sing about
e. and to make sure that the songs chosen reflect this particular congregation's concerns.

There are lots of other steps to take once these elements are in place, but first things first.

MODELS IN THE MIND

I would like to share with you some experiences that I have had, mainly reflections from my travels across the United States. A number of years ago I attended a terrible eucharistic liturgy. The music was poor, the ritual action seemed out of place, the assembly was excluded from participation. Because the liturgy was celebrated by a national organization that will remain unidentified, I went to comment to those who had been involved in the planning. Before I could say anything, however, they exclaimed, "Wasn't that the greatest celebration you have ever been to?" They were serious. I bit my tongue, mouthed some bland niceties, and reflected on the experience.

The next year the same organization celebrated a liturgy near my home diocese of Richmond, and this time the eucharist was extremely simple, the music accompaniment by harp and flute, and there was strong sung participation. It contained all the values that I held dear. After the liturgy I met someone from New York who said, "Wasn't that liturgy terrible? It was so bland." At first I was dumbfounded. I wondered whether there is no such thing as objectively good liturgy. Is everything simply a subjective reflection of some previous liturgical experience that we have called "good" or "meaningful," which we have developed as a mindset model for comparison? This was the question, and it was a question that intrigued me.

The first response to that question is clear. Liturgy cannot be judged as *effective* except in relation to God. Worship is about the praise and thanks given to God, and to God alone. Nothing else really counts. But certain experiences of worship do seem to "work" better than others at including the community and expressing its heartfelt praise and thanks, and those of us who are "responsible" for preparing and directing the ritual celebration need to be aware of the dynamics at work when ritual takes place, if for no other reason than to avoid obvious mistakes.

As I began to formulate my reflections on such experiences, I noticed that there was a style of celebration that emphasized communication. The goal of the liturgy was "meaning," making sure that people understood what was being said. The presider's vestments in this kind of liturgy were often just an alb and stole, the room was usually plain or modern. The music chosen for this style of worship expressed the meaning of the text in a straightforward manner, as does Suzanne Toolen's "I Am the Bread of Life," with its rising refrain, "And I will raise you up . . . on the last day." It is impossible to sing that melody without singing the meaning of the text. Father Gene Walsh was a great advocate of this style of celebration and trained many priests in it.

Then I began to notice some reactions to this "plain" style, especially at the Notre Dame Center for Pastoral Liturgy. A number of people, John Gallen and Aidan Kavanagh among them, stressed the importance of ritual. "Do what is in the book," we have all heard John Gallen insist. Marking such celebrations are the use of incense and bells and full, rich vestments. Sacred Heart Chapel at Notre Dame, with its updated but still ornate nineteenth-century architecture, fits right into this style of celebration. And so does Germanic hymnody. Hymnody is predictable: you know how the melody is going to end, even if you can't follow the meaning of the text. You can sing ritualistically, with certainty, and not necessarily attend to the meaning.

And when I recognized these two styles of celebration, I began looking at other liturgical styles. I discovered a monastic style where the key element is not meaning or stability, but a call to enter into another place, a call to otherworldly holiness. Everything about this liturgical style is countercultural. The building that serves as its setting is severe in design, modeled on the clean Scandinavian lines of buildings designed by Frank Kacmarcik or Ed Sövik. The priestly gestures are very quiet, internal, impersonal, and intense. The music is ethereal, like Gregorian chant. It lifts you out of the existing experience and space and places you in another experience.

And on the West Coast, especially in California, I began seeing a more flamboyant, dramatic, entertaining style. At first I was a bit put off, thinking that such liturgy was too theatrical, too dramatic. But the more I examined this style, the more I realized that what was happening was an initial appeal to the sense of entertainment, the sense of delight. It was quite different from an approach that begins with a call to holiness, or stability, or meaning. This style appeals to the most common characteristic of our times, the need to be entertained.

I watched and listened to Don Osuna at St. Francis de Sales Cathedral in Oakland and Jake Empereur at the Institute for Spirituality and Worship in Berkeley. I thought about the former liturgical dress of a bishop, topped by a tall miter, or the processional vesture of a cardinal—the orange-scarlet cappa magna trimmed in ermine—and I pictured processions accompanied by a corps of servers with candles or "torches." I thought back to the Tenebrae service in the seminary when the lights were turned out and we banged our *Libers* on the pews to imitate thunder, and I realized that the liturgy has traditionally been filled with appeals to the sense of delight, to "entertainment" values in that sense. Dance, drama, and music close to the popular culture all enter into this style of liturgy.

At this point I felt that I had discovered four basic styles of celebration: the Monastic, with its call to holiness; the Ritualistic, with its promise of a faithful God; the Communicative, with its pledge to provide meaning; and the Dramatic, with its desire to trigger the level of delight.

And then I went to St. Augustine Parish in Washington, D.C., where African-American music rings through the church from both choir and congregation, where gestures and spontaneous outcries provide a unique celebration that fits none of the other categories. Then I remembered the Hispanic "mariachi liturgy" in San Antonio, and the Vietnamese 6:00 A.M. liturgy in California, and the "social action liturgies" where special communities gather to sing and pray about racial injustice, AIDS, and the homeless. And I realized that there is a fifth style of celebration, which I've called Homogenous. In this Homogenous style the assembly is so united around a given issue or item that it dominates the style of celebration, music, and ritual that takes place in that liturgy.

ELEMENTS OF STYLE

Since I first came across these five approaches to liturgy, I have tested them against a number of celebrations that I have attended, and it is clear that the first, most controlling factor about any celebration style is the building in which the celebration takes place. A Gothic cathedral demands a ritual celebration; a communicative style celebration appears ridiculous in that space. And a modern confrontational-seating church calls for a communicative style liturgy; when the presider and the music become otherwise, they just don't seem to fit. And so forth. Such "out-of-place" styles are true not only for the music chosen, but the way that the presider approaches the assembly.

The second thing that I noticed was that the music of the first four styles has a certain progression from ancient to contemporary. Beginning with the monastic model, with no trace of any contemporary popular sounds in the music, there is a spectrum that ends at the dramatic style, where contemporary popular sounds are unabashedly evident in the music. The middle two styles mix popular secular musical sounds with other kinds of music. In the ritualistic style those sounds are more hidden, but present nevertheless, while the communicative has glimpses and peeks of contemporary popular sounds appearing throughout.

The third thing I noticed was that one style is not better than any other; the "fit" depends on the building, the congregation, the presider, and the musicians (in that order).

So with these models in mind, I went back to my early experience and discovered that the liturgy I had rejected out of hand was in a more dramatic style than I was used to, but the following year's liturgy was in the communicative style with which I had grown up.

It all seemed so clear, now. There is not one style of liturgy that is objectively correct, but several, at least. And I then reflected that any one of these liturgical styles carried to an extreme can become a caricature; and each of them tends to serve as a cor-

rective for the others. If ritual becomes the only element in liturgy, for instance, we lose meaning. Or if meaning becomes the
only element, then we over-intellectualize. If the call to counter-
culture holiness is all we ever hear, we lose sight of the human,
the ordinary person, and so forth.

Somehow, over the past twenty-five years, when liturgical
changes have been allowed to find their own level of development—and this is especially true of our musical evolution—the
ebb-and-flow of different liturgical leaders in the United States
has pushed us toward examining the limitations of each of our
styles of celebration and has provided us with correctives, re-
directives.

How, then do you apply all this to congregational song? Perhaps you have to step out into the light, go someplace where the
key was not lost, in order to find what was lost somewhere else.
If congregations are not singing, the problem may not lie in the
song or the singers; it may be that the building is not right for this
song, or the style of worship may be at odds with the needs of the
singers. But we may only discover what the problem really is by
stepping out into the light and looking at the way other people
worship, and where they worship, and how they sing.

The five styles I have observed and shared in can offer clergy
and musicians and other liturgical leaders a way to determine
which style of celebration is dominant in their parish. They can
also suggest "balances" or correctives, especially in the area of
musical repertoire, that might be drawn from the other styles of
celebration in order to develop a rich, more complete approach to
the worship of this gathered assembly.

FIVE

PARTICIPATION:
IS IT WORTH THE EFFORT?

First, let me explain the problem that, in my opinion, is at the very heart of the invitation to "full, conscious, and active participation": how should we understand this participation?

The participation affirmed by Vatican II was a magnificent victory over a certain type of theology that reigned in the nineteenth century and in the spirit of Vatican I. Vatican I replaced "ecclesiology," as Yves Congar says, with "hierarchology." In a word, the church was considered essentially as a hierarchy. Pope Gregory XVI (1836-1846) had written that the church "is an unequal society in which God destined some people to govern and others to obey."[1] Pius X, who was indeed a holy pope, made the following almost unbelievable assertions in his 1906 encyclical *Vehementer Nos*:

> The church is an unequal society, including two categories of persons: the pastors and the flock, those who belong to the hierarchy and the multitude of the faithful. These two categories are distinct. In the pastors alone abides the right and the necessary authority to promote and lead the members toward the aim of the society. As to the multitude [of the faithful] the only right they have is to let themselves be led and to follow the pastors as a docile (submitted) flock.

In this hierarchology, the people ("submitted flock") are invited to attend, to watch, to admire what the priests are celebrating. It is exactly against this kind of the liturgy that Vatican II, in 1963, affirmed that the faithful should participate "fully, consciously, and actively."

Is that enough? It was enough for 1963. But in 1965 Vatican II defined the church also as a *koinonia*,[2] the communion of the children of God. Paul VI underlined "the communal character of the church" in that there is a "brotherhood which unites in the same communion all the believers in Christ."[3] This ecclesiology changes the face of the liturgy: as the church is a *koinonia*, the liturgical celebrations must also be a *koinonia*, a communion. In other words, liturgy must really be a celebration of the whole community.

Who celebrates the Mass? In the past we answered: "The priest." Today we respond: "The community." Who presides at the celebration? In the past we answered: "The priest." Today we must answer: "Christ." The role of the priest is not diminished. He is part of the celebrating community, rendering to it the ministry of presidency, being the soul of its *koinonia*.

Does the word "participation" express the totality of the celebration of the faithful? To participate means "to have or take a part." Now the congregation does not "take a part," whether small or big, in the celebration, but it has to celebrate the totality of the liturgy. Each believer, having the royal dignity of baptism, celebrates according to his or her rank. The faithful do not "take a part" in the celebration of the faithful. Together, in the *koinonia* of the Body of Christ, they celebrate the Father.

In my opinion, this vision of the church-communion is the greatest change in our age. It introduces the greatest changes in our liturgy. Finally, it reflects in a perfect way the Gospel of the Lord who affirms: "You are all on the same level as brothers and sisters" (Mt 23:8).[4]

Message of the Numbers

We might wonder if this question is not merely a theological one. Is it of any interest for the musical program I am preparing for next Sunday? Let me quote some numbers that speak for themselves.

Those people who in 1963 were twenty years old or more, who knew the liturgy of pre-Vatican II, who longed for the reform, worked for it, and obtained practically everything they asked for, today represent the people of maturity. The others, let us say the young people of the church, have resolved in their own way the problem of "full, conscious, and active participation" in the liturgy: they participate no more, or they participate rarely. In Germany, for instance, in the past years the number of "churchgoers" among Protestants went down from thirteen to two percent, and among Catholic from fifty-nine to fourteen percent. These numbers may be approximately the same in other nations of western Europe. Statistics for the United States also indicate significantly diminished regular attendance at church. Recent polls put Catholic attendance at Mass at approximately fifty percent. This means that the "docile and submitted flock" which, according to St. Pius X, is supposed to follow the hierarchy (or to follow the music director) is reduced to two percent in European Catholic churches and to about fifty percent in American Catholic parishes.

No new song, no new liturgical trick will bring back those not at all interested by the "re-form" of the liturgy or even by its actual "form." The statistics seem to indicate that there is an immense problem in our way of celebration as well as in their way of participation.

Two Pseudo-Solutions

There are two incomplete ways of dealing with the problem of participation. They both arrive at an incomplete solution.

The first way would be to insist on mere external participation, for example, by inviting the people to sing louder or sing more, by demanding more organ or more guitar, more choir or more congregational singing. But liturgical participation always includes an interior dimension. Exterior noise, whatever its musical quality may be, is not necessarily the sign of the best participation. There can be excellent celebration without singing at all.

The second way would be to insist on mere interior participation, for instance, by inviting only interior prayer. But there can be perfect interior prayer without participation in the celebration of the whole assembly. True participation must include body and soul in the whole of the celebration of the church-communion.[5]

The important question is the following. Supposing that the whole community participates exteriorly by all possible means and interiorly by an interior prayer, how could the community still realize a "fuller, more conscious and more active participation" in the liturgy?

Let us examine now what could be done today in accordance with the rubrical laws, what might be a desirable evolution. There are always innumerable problems that involve not only the theology of the church, but also the sensibility of the faithful (*pius sensus fidelium*). Within the limits of this article, I offer a few considerations of dreams. You may add your own ideas. We are always allowed to dream.

The Heartbeat of the Eucharistic Action

The "full" participation requires the celebration of the "full" liturgy. Vatican II teaches that "the eucharistic action is the very heartbeat of the congregation of the faithful." Because of the shortage of priests, however, the eucharist cannot be celebrated in a great number of communities, both in the United States and in Europe. In the mission countries we often find missionaries who have to serve one hundred and twenty stations in the bush. If such a priest celebrates five Masses (two on Saturday and three on Sunday), there are still one hundred and nineteen communities that must celebrate the Day of the Lord without this "heartbeat." Even in Europe there are priests who are in charge of ten or twelve churches.

If this situation is the will of the Lord, blessed is he! He is always right. But if it is only the result of a human disposition erecting barriers to access to the priesthood, what can we say? How can a person survive without a heartbeat? How can a community survive without this eucharistic heartbeat?

Of course, I believe in the necessity of the witness given by celibate priests for the Kingdom. At the same time, I believe that each community has the right to the ministers that the community needs. Because it is always suitable to quote the word of God, let us recall that according to Titus 1:6-9, the conditions for access to the priesthood are those of Christian life: the presbyter must be blameless, husband of but one wife ("man of one love," as we would say today), not quick-tempered, not given to much wine, not violent, hospitable (in order to welcome the community), self-controlled, upright . . .

There is also the very real problem of the place of women in liturgical celebration. It is difficult to speak about full, conscious, and active participation if half the community is excluded from the sanctuary. If that situation is the result of the will of the Lord, blessed be he! He is always right. But if the situation is only the result of a male dominated church, what can we say?

Let us also add a word about the presidency of the eucharist. In the early church the general practice seems to have been that the one who presided over the community also presided over the eucharist.[7] This principle could resolve the painful situation of communities that currently can celebrate the eucharist only once or twice a year.

The Eucharistic Prayer

The instruction *Inaestimabile Donum* (3 April, 1980) affirms that "the proclamation of the eucharistic prayer is, of its nature, the high point of the whole celebration." It should be thus the high point of the participation of the congregation.

This prayer is pronounced by the priest alone, stressing the unique role of the ministerial priesthood. It is pronounced by the priest in the name of the whole congregation. In a beautiful way Guerric d'Igny (thirteenth century) explains: "The priest does not consecrate alone, but the whole assembly consecrates and sanctifies with him."[8]

In order to express the participation of the people, we have in our Roman Liturgy the Sanctus, the Memorial Acclamation, and the Great Amen. At the very least, these should always be treated as acclamations. Tradition has given us other acclamations as well. In the Coptic liturgy, for instance, the people intervene at the very heart of the eucharistic prayer with acclamations like "Amen, we believe! That is true!" or "Amen, amen, amen! We confess and give you glory!" I know from personal experience that these acclamations, accompanied by thirty cymbals, make a wonderful noise of joyous thanksgiving. It seems that in Egypt to be pious means to clash cymbals, whereas in our countries to be pious means to bow our heads and to be silent. Is there need of more communal joy in our celebrations?

In certain celebrations the whole assembly recites the eucharistic prayer. Yves Congar writes on this matter:

The entire liturgical assembly is celebrating and consecrating, but it would be an ecclesiological error and a liturgical heresy to ask the whole assembly to say the words of eucharistic consecration. The assembly has a president who ministers as president. And still the whole assembly is entirely sacerdotal and celebrant.[9]

Let me add an observation. The account of the Last Supper is like a reading of the word of God. Nobody would think that the community, in order to express its participation in the gospel, should read it along with the lector. This line of thinking, by the way, is valid also for concelebration when all the priests say the eucharistic prayer together in a loud voice. In so doing, the distinction beween priest and congregation is stressed, thereby destroying the very unity that the concelebration should express. This practice also diminishes the importance of the prayers of praise and thanksgiving that are an integral part of the eucharistic prayer.

Celebration of the Word

There are a number of problems pertaining to the celebration of the word. Let us mention a few.

Preparation. No one should dare celebrate the word of God without having first studied it. John Chrysostom contemplated for an entire week the gospel about which he was to preach on a given Sunday.[10] This kind of serious preparation is the true price to be paid in order to participate fully and consciously in the word of God.

Penitential Rite; General Intercessions. These prayers should be based on the word. They normally belong to the congregation to prepare.

Readers. Each passage of the word of God should have a reader who is carefully chosen, well-trained, and fully prepared. To be at ease in proclaiming the word of God, the reader should know it almost by heart.

Homily. The success of a celebration is measured ordinarily by the quality of the homily. The major criterion for judging the quality of a homily is that it be rooted in the proclaimed word of God. The priest, as presider, is normally responsible for the homily. This does not imply that he has to speak at all times. In group Masses, such as Masses for children, for instance, the women and men who have the responsbility for the religious education of children are also the ones who can give the best homilies to them.

Liturgy of the Hours

The liturgy of the hours is not the prayer of the monks, priests, or sisters, but first of all the prayer of the Christian community to which monks, priests, and sisters belong. This was the tradition of the ancient church. It remains the teaching of the church today. "The Church's praise [prayer] is not to be considered the exclusive possession of clerics and monks either by its origin or by its nature, but belongs to the whole Christian community."[11]

Here the question is pointed: Does the Christian community, does the parish community, "participate" fully, consciously, and actively in this prayer which is its own prayer? Even more pointed is the question: Do we really desire both to appear and actually to be, in the eyes of the world, a praying people? It is a fact that in Makurdi, Nigeria, the Christian community at a particular college organizes communal prayer five times each day in order to be praying as often as the Moslem majority prays. I know well that in our beloved church many heartening things are happening. But we must admit that we still have a long way to go in order to be seen by the world as a praying community.

Participation of All Art Forms

As musicians, we naturally think that music, especially singing, is the ordinary way of participation. Surely singing is an important way; it is not, however, the only way. All other art forms should be included: painting, sculpture, and especially for the children and young people, dance. If liturgical dance is offered with dignity and at the right time and place, it can be a wonderful moment of full, conscious, and active worship.[12] Of course, dancing demands a high price: preparation, rehearsal, dignity, and interior prayer. Experience shows, however, that our young people are generous enough to pay that high price for the love of the wonderful Lord, in order to participate really fully, that is with soul and body, in the adoration of God.[13]

Our greatest dignity is to be baptized and, therefore, to belong to the priestly, prophetic, and royal people of God. Our greatest joy as musicians is to open a path of beauty for our community toward our marvelous Lord. We cannot lead our congregation to this full, conscious, and active participation if we do not participate ourselves. In other words, we cannot lead the sung prayer of our assembly if we do not pray ourselves. We cannot open this path of beauty if we do not walk in it ourselves. As Eucharistic Prayer II states: "Lord, we thank you for counting us worthy to stand and serve you"—with music and with beauty!

Notes

1. See L. Deiss, *Persons in Liturgical Celebrations* (Cincinnati: World Library Publications, 1978) 1-4 and note 3, p. 61; also Yves Congar, *Le Concile de Vatican II,* Théologie historique, vol. 71 (Paris: Beauchesne, 1984) 12-16.

2. *Koinonia* is the technical word in the New Testament, in patristic writings, and in the theology of the Middle Ages to signify the life and grace we have in common (*kolvos*) with God. See *Theologisches Worterbuch zum Neuen Testament*, vol. 3 (1938) 789-809.

3. Even though there are still different ministries (see 1 Cor 12:5), including the ministry of the hierarchy.

4. See Hans Küng, *Vie Eternelle* (Paris: Ed. du Seuil, 1985) 260.

5. Decree on the Ministry and Life of Priests, no. 5.

6. See the excellent study of H.-M. Legrand, "La Présidence de l'eucharistie selon la tradition ancienne," *Spiritus* 56 (December 1977) 409-431.

7. Sermo 7 (PL 185:57).

8. Congar, *Le Concile de Vatican* II 113; see also *Inaestimabile Donum*, no. 4.

9. See John G. Baldovin, "Concelebration: Problem of Symbolic Roles in the Church," *Worship* 59 (1985) 32-47.

10. Homily on John, Homily 11:1 (PG 59:77).

11. General Instruction on the Liturgy of the Hours, no. 270; see also nos. 20, 21, 26, and 33.

12. Lucien Deiss and Gloria Weyman, *Dance for the Lord* (Cincinnati: World Library Publications, 1977); Thomas Kane and others, *Introducing Dance in Christian Worship* (Washington, D.C.: The Pastoral Press, 1984).

13. Lucien Deiss and Gloria Weyman, *Liturgical Dance* (videotape and book) (Phoenix: North American Liturgy Resources, 1984).

PERFORMANCE vs. PARTICIPATION

SIX

THE CONGREGATION'S ACTIVE PARTICIPATION IS PERFORMANCE

When we speak of performance and participation in liturgical prayer, we often express the need for more active participation by the congregation, and we note the existence of revised standards of performance for pastoral musicians. We recognize the dual service the liturgical musician must now perform: the facilitation of the congregation's singing, and the performance of more complex music of beauty to aid the congregation's prayer at other times. When problems surface in this area, they are often problems of balance—balance between the choir's "performance" and the congregation's "participation." "The choir sings too much!" "We never hear anything beautiful from the choir anymore!"

I'd like to address this problem by offering you a new set of glasses, as it were, with which to view what we all do together when we celebrate a ritual. When we look through these glasses, we have to drop, for a time, the conventional usage of the words "performance" and "participation." Underlying this viewpoint there's a hunch that if we can change our perception of what constitutes the major symbols and symbolic actions of the liturgy and if we pay attention to the spirited performance of *all* these symbols, a balance between the activity of the choir, instrumentalists, readers, ushers, dancers, and "ordinary" members of the assembly will naturally and more frequently be found.

We humans, by God's design, are embodied beings and as such we know things and individuals and, indeed, God, only through what our senses perceive— through what we feel, hear, see, smell, touch. The husky voice of a neighbor or the energetic dancing of the kids next door are aural and visual events, which, in combination with many other sensory data, can reveal to me the person who is my neighbor and the people who are the kids next door. We call these sensory events symbols. They are perceptible things that allow me to make contact with realities I cannot directly perceive.

Prayer, or private conversation with the Lord who is present to me, is also symbolic. Some examples of prayer symbols are images such as the cross or a tall mountain or a visualized story from the Scriptures; a series of sounds— our music; or an action such as a greeting of peace exchanged between Christians. A Christian liturgical celebration, like all public ritual events, is a complex symbolic activity in which all people involved, including the "ordinary" members of the congregations (formerly thought of as "participants") are symbol makers, *performers*, if you will, active agents constructing something visible, audible, or tangible through which we may experience the presence of God in the church.

One of the fundamental symbols in Christian liturgy is the assembly itself. All who take the trouble to get their bodies into the church, who take the trouble to be seen and heard, and to be touched, render a holy service because by their very presence and action they constitute the symbol that is the *church assembled*.

I would say that some details of this symbol are relatively unimportant, such as our fatness or thinness, or the resonance or tightness of our voices. What is important is that we are seen and heard and touched. Of equal importance, however, is the measure of the Spirit's life we have allowed to flower within us, the level and intensity of joy, peace, faith, hope, and love we bring to the event. This inner life, built up of God's gift and our toil, decisions, and sufferings, is reflected in our faces and voices and gestures. This is what can transform a mere visual image of Becky, Sam, and the children in the first pew into an icon radiating the presence of the wonderful Lord among us all. The *active participation* of the so-called "ordinary" members of the congregation is itself a *performance*. We are always, as the title of Bernard Huijbers' book proclaims, *The Performing Audience*, though again, the conventional connotations of "audience" do not apply in this particular instance.

In addition to the symbol of the church assembled, the congregation helps to construct the symbol of the word. For it is the *hearing of the proclaimed word* that completes the symbol of the word. The assembly is essential to the construction of the symbol of the meal, for it is *the partaking of the bread and wine* that completes the symbol of the eucharistic meal, complementing the elements and prayers of the priest. Performance and participation in ritual are two aspects of the same reality.

Some symbols in the liturgy require more art and craft than others. The one who proclaims the word should have, among other qualities, a good voice and must know how to use it; just as the dancer should have a disciplined and responsive body; the singer and instrumentalist should be musically gifted and trained; and the priest celebrant for any assembly should be a gifted and trained presider. But the symbols of word, image, and sound that these servants of the community construct are no different in kind than those crafted by the congregation; everyone involved is constantly *performing*. Needless to say, it is equally important for this group of special symbol-makers to have an active life of the Spirit that must infuse their art.

The sight of people processing forward to receive communion is just as significant a symbolic act as a choir's "recital" piece at communion time. Perhaps we don't watch each other in church with any sense of contemplative wonder. Maybe we haven't given enough thought to the concrete ways in which we construct symbols such as the *sharing in the body and blood of the Lord*. We grumble if communion takes some time, yet isn't this what we've come for? Isn't this the banquet of the Lord? Is it so out of line if the actual eating takes more than ten minutes? We need to set our creative minds to work to devise concrete ways to make this activity and others truly dignified and human events capable of mediating our experience of the Lord in his church for us. And while we're on the subject, what about some careful thought directed to the symbolism of the *one loaf* and the importance of the fraction rite, and the reception of both elements: food *and* drink.

Clearly we have not yet come to know all there is to know about the ritual we call the eucharist. We certainly have a lot to learn about the symbolic structure of the ceremony. And, unfortunately, as it is sometimes performed, the liturgy not only fails to give us proper clues but gives us false clues as to what we are about when we celebrate.

A change of viewpoint regarding the performance role of everyone present at the liturgy and greater attention to the symbolic building blocks of the ritual would be positive steps forward. This would place the question of the balance between *performance* and *participation* in its proper context.

SEVEN

TWO BECOME ONE: PERFORMANCE AND PARTICIPATION

Each of us brings all kinds of unspoken expectations to worship. Inner-city prophets want to see proclamation and preaching unpack powerful demands from the word of God for justice, mercy, and community. High church types seek musical splendor—brass choir and tympani supplying driving syncopation to this swell of massed voices. Theologically sensitive partisans of "renewal" most want to see all individuals in the assembly open their mouths and *join in*. Still others look for "mystery," the "presence," the sense of the ineffable associated with the age-old sacrifice of the Mass. Most of us represent a blend of these and other attitudes.

While none of these orientations is "wrong" in itself, each carries a different emphasis in the balance between reason and feeling, word and rite, participation and performance. Inescapably, in common prayer, we exist in a tension between a pole that represents *quality* and a pole that represents *shared responsibility*. Thorough exploration of this question can uncover a balance between these two poles.

One issue seems to be more fundamental than others in getting a perspective on the balance in question. Older generations seemed to relate to the Sunday experience in terms of being filled up: taking their empty human shells to church, they received grace. But so much of the new theology has helped us perceive that this is only half the story. The other half can be glimpsed in various phrases in the documents of Vatican II: Christ enlivens the baptized through the gift of the Spirit; this Spirit animates "all their works, prayers, and apostolic endeavors, their ordinary married and family life, their daily labor, their mental and physical relaxation"; and all this is offered to the Father "along with the Lord's Body" (Vatican II: Dogmatic Constitution on the Church, no. 34). Thus the meaning of the Sunday assembly is not alone that of bestowing the worshipers with holy gifts; it is just as fundamentally a privileged moment in which to testify to the Holy Spirit that is in them.

It is clear from constantly repeated instances that the enormous reluctance of many Sunday Christians to engage in any deep or challenging participation in worship through song, gesture, or spoken word is rooted in a preconciliar vision of worship. "Look! Get on with it," they have said to me, either directly or in so many words. Get on with it: Say the Mass, give me the sacrament, fill me up, and leave me alone. It is one of the real sadnesses of this period of renewal that there seem to be bishops and priests in the American Church who are content to do just that. And so worship in spirit and in truth—characterized by freedom and joyful urgency—seldom emerges.

There is tension between the liturgy as God's gesture and the liturgy as the believer's gesture. Theologians have long asked: "Is the liturgy formative of community, or does the liturgy presuppose a community of believers?" In a certain way it is both. As the activity that hands on to a new day the stories of God in Jesus and the sacraments that he guided the church to elaborate in his name, the liturgy is formative of community. Any community that no longer accepts these gifts cannot really be called Christian. But the acceptance and celebration of these gifts by themselves do not satisfy the *full* point of the liturgy. Prayer is not so many words read, pages turned, songs sung, gestures enacted, symbols used, sacred objects touched, and so forth. These actions alone are not liturgy, but merely rite. *Liturgy* is lived and living dialogue of human beings with divine beings and among one another—a dialogue that perpetually has the power to make unforseen demands.

When this dialogue is lost, rite easily becomes ritualism. Ritualism by itself can become idolatrous if, for example, an individual were more concerned with observing certain rites than with meeting the living God manifested in those rites. Such observance worships the worship forms, not the living God, and thereby merits the name of idolatry.

Christopher Kiesling attacks our culture's "consumerism" as the force perverting our worship. "The consumer regards liturgy as a product or service to be received, rather than as an event which he or she is to create with others." The "consumer" doesn't understand participation—and often doesn't have very high expectations of performance either, although the "consumer" *perceives* Mass as performance. "Participation vs. performance" may signify the gap between turning pages in a missalette on the one hand and experiencing an awesome event of artful prayer on the other; but even more fundamentally, these words express primary realities of Christian experience.

"Participation" expresses first of all the reality of a community of people together. Unlike the Hindu shrine, the Buddhist zendo, or the Muslim call to worship, the Christian assembly is not simply a gathering of individuals to make their personal prayers in a common place inhabited by all. The Christian mystery is the mystery of a people.

The idea represents an impressive challenge for all of us. Yet this is the revealed plan: this earthly place will be transformed. It is a task not for occasional religious heroes, not even for a hidden God alone; rather, it is a task for those called to it—called to achieve the mystery God has preached in Jesus Christ. This means that the Sunday assembly must have a pragmatic air about it. The gathering of the assembly must be something more than the exorcism of a fear of the mortal sin of nonattendance. It is a time for challenge, recommitment, practical assessment, bonding together for the struggle.

"Performance," in the context of liturgy, does not occur in a personal vacuum—as a kind of esthetic eruption without a context. "Performance" is measured and judged precisely in terms of being a response to a preliminary initiative of God within the church. Yet when God speaks within the church, it is on the lips of living men and women. The meaning of the measured yet abundant beauty that invests our words and gestures with glory and power—the meaning of "performance"—is that it is the garb

of the holy, of that which is most authentic. The words of the
Gospel, like the songs of the believers, are not messages for our
reasoning minds alone. They are words, gestures, and melodies—repeated through the centuries—that create an environment that fosters commitment, pushing us beyond the surface of
our fears and providing us an alphabet for hope. We are in
continuity with ages of hope.

The community is called to hear the prophetic word of God in
the Scriptures and to receive the word as a vision for life. Yet no
single reading of the word exhausts its power, no single preaching exhausts its meaning. We barely scratch the surface in our
celebrations. The prophetic word of God is *expansive*—it unfolds
in silence. So many biblical images of God's power are clothed in
silence: the Spirit brooding over Genesis, the stillness of Elijah's
encounter with God on Mount Horeb, the midnight birth of the
savior, the watching in the upper room until Pentecost. And the
silence is followed by an explosive and creative transformation of
the world that flows out of the power of the word grown to its
fullness in stillness and waiting.

There are many voices of silence. One of its vestures is music.
Max Picard claims that music is an extension of silence: "The
sound of music is not, like the sound of words, opposed but
parallel to silence. It is as though the sound of music were being
drawn over the surface of silence." We need to experience this
power of music to unlock the hidden senses of the prophetic
words of worship—the power to unravel the tangled strands of
meaning that underlie words of faith and prayer.

For the word of God to be *life*, there has to be an inner speaking
by God that testifies to the saving power of the church. This inner
voice is the anointed silence that unwraps the meaning of the
sacred words for us. Most of us have known occasional moments
in which the brilliance of a preacher, the touching beauty of a
choir's singing, or the magnetic unity of a congregation caught
up in enthusiastic song touched something very deep inside us.
It is foolish to run away from such moments—to treat them
lightly. Like Mary in Luke 2:19, we need to treasure these things
and ponder them in our hearts. What is unutterable in the mere
toil of words remains real for the heart in the region of silence.

Without this silence, holy words can be information, but not salvation.

What we mean by secularity today is not a *rejection* of God, but rather an *affirmation* of God as penetrating the whole of life. It is the assertion that there are not two worlds, one small holy one where God dwells in a golden tabernacle and another large secular one where humankind has unbridled sovereignty. It is the affirmation that there is only one world in which the one God is met in creation, in prophecy, in loving encounters and in the compassionate rebuilding of the earth—and all this is summarized and proclaimed in liturgy.

To be what it really has to be—the gathering up of all the fragments of life—our liturgical prayer must confront our eyes and ears with an authentic sense of what is churning in the continuing creation of the world. Even if we do not know how to obey God's voice in its midst or how to interpret his message within it, nonetheless God is present in it all. We are too quick to dismiss the changes of the world as unsuited to divine communication, too quick to dismiss God's surprises in our world as unsuited to good taste. If history is any lesson, however, God will not be easily domesticated by our categories of tastefulness. God will dance and make new songs, will find new media and stick with them until they shine with the rewards of skillful discipline. And if we wish to dance with God, God's joy will be the greater.

From these perspectives, it is reasonable to assert that the tension between excellent performance of rites and fullsome participation of hearts is healthy and inescapable. We have to do the best we can to realize both dimensions: both are integral to genuine worship.

In Christian worship we are called to express our personal gifts fully and deeply, but in the context of and for the sake of a community of varied personalities. We are called to repeat in a new age and language and culture the old stories and relive the old memories, but to do so with freshness and creativity so that they live with an unpredictable power. We are called to challenge one another with the vision of a coming age of justice and love that at present lies beyond our reach, but to do so within a celebration of thanks that so much of the coming age has already touched our lives. To realize these demands, we need to learn how to express a plurality of seemingly contrary values: solidarity/conviction; searching/simplicity; creativity/fidelity.

The creative disbelief of Nietzche in the last century has helped many theologians understand the dialetical tension within which the contemporary worshiper stands. This is representative of Nietzche's challenge to the church: "For me to believe in their redeemer, Christians would have to sing better songs, and they would have to look more redeemed." Such a complaint helps us see that the tension between performance and participation cannot be collapsed; they must be melded. Performance—the excellence of singing and saying and doing—and participation—the individual's surrender to the transforming work of the worshiping community—must coalesce. One without the other can only be either estheticism or boosterism. Together, they become the enfleshment of a mystery that remains age after age both challenge and promise, surrender and consolation.

Note

1. Christopher Kiesling, "Liturgy and Consumerism," *Worship* 52:4 (July 1978) 365.

Joseph Gelineau

EIGHT

BALANCING PERFORMANCE AND PARTICIPATION

The church was born of sound and word. The Acts of the Apostles tells us that on the day of Pentecost there was a great noise and the multitude gathered; Peter spoke; and three thousand people were baptized. This was a model of "sound" performance and believing participation, and I believe the "balancing" was rather successful.

In this founding event there were two things: sound and gathering. These elements concern us in each and every liturgy. After the large gathering on the day of Pentecost, we read in Acts: "They devoted themselves to the apostles' instruction and the communal life, to the breaking of bread and the prayers . . . praising God, and winning the approval of all the people" (Acts 2:42ff.). Vatican II's Constitution on the Sacred Liturgy, after citing this text, continues: "Never since has the church neglected to gather for the celebration of the Paschal Mystery" (no. 6).

Christians are first and foremost people who gather together. This trait really impressed the pagans of the first century. In fact, the word *ecclesia* means convocation and gathering. So in this we have both a sign and a sacrament: the church is a communion.

But for us musicians, who are people of sound and ear, there is a more specific reason for gathering. Indeed, why must Christians gather? First, to listen to the word of God and respond to it; and, second, to give thanks and praise in celebrating the Lord's Supper.

We listen to the word. St. Paul wrote to the Colossians: "Let the word of Christ, in all its richness, find a home in you. In wisdom made perfect, instruct and admonish one another. Sing gratefully to God from your hearts in psalms, hymns, and inspired songs" (Col 3:16). From this very rich text I will draw only one thing for the moment: "Instruct one another." This means that the word of God comes to us through human lips, and that God does not speak to me if no other person speaks to me. The message of the Gospel presupposes a gathering, and the first task of any production of sound in the liturgy is to carry the word of God to the ears of those who believe. This can, of course, be done in a great number of forms.

Then, second, we must elicit the response in faith of the gathering to the proclaimed word. This response is sometimes an acknowledgement of faith; sometimes supplication and request; sometimes an action of thanksgiving and praise.

Thus, Christian liturgy was born as the dialogue of God and God's people. For it is the Lord who speaks to his people when we read the Gospel, and it is the same Lord who is present in his people when we sing the psalms. As Psalm 21 says, "God dwells in the praises of Israel." And all of this performance and participation takes place in the gathering.

My remarks thus far have all been to draw your attention to the necessity for us to *welcome* each other to celebrate the liturgy. We cannot sing together comfortably if we do not look at each other and manifest our joy of being together.

In all this, where is music? It is everywhere, for the Christian liturgy was born singing. It is praise. I know that in stating this I may be blasting the notion of music. But it was by design that I spoke of sound and the gathering. For if the announcement of the word were reduced to merely communicating the notional content of the message, the liturgy would be useless in this age of the printed word; it would suffice to read your Bible. And if prayer were reduced to saying things to God, it would not be necessary to speak aloud or even to gather.

As soon as we gather, as soon as we celebrate, a certain music is already there—in the resonance of a sanctuary, be it delightful or annoying; it is in the timbre of a voice, pleasant or unpleasant; it is in the collective murmur of a crowd reciting a prayer. To those of you who like to record sounds: it's extraordinary, a crowd that is praying. And for those who are technically minded, music is also in the diaphragms of the loudspeakers; in the vibrations of bells, and so forth.

I want to say this: the church musician who thinks only of the notes and the score risks some great pitfalls. For it is often *other* sound values in a celebration that unconsciously have more influence on the psychology of the participants. In contrast to the eye, which chooses what it wants to see, the ear receives everything at once: the words, the music, the footsteps of people moving about, the slamming door, the microphone that crackles, and so forth. These are very important things for the celebration. It takes very little to hinder prayer, but it takes but a single beautiful sound to exalt it.

There are many ways to analyze the performance-participation relationship. I would like to suggest that the balancing presupposes three "tunings." A musician knows what it means for a note to be in tune. The first tuning is that of the relationship among the members of the congregation. Every sound, every word establishes a certain relationship among those who speak. The primary function of the human word is not to say something, but to enter into a relationship with someone in a certain way. All who open their mouths in the liturgy must not forget this. The second tuning is that of the personal attitude, at the same time bodily, psychic, spiritual. The third tuning is that of the collective symbolic action represented by the rite.

One example of sound and word is the proclamation. The proclamation is a vocal gesture by which an individual makes an announcement to a gathered public. We have a typical example in the liturgy: the preface. The preface is the open and public proclamation of the wonders of God. It is a public attestation that God has saved each of us. The relationship of the speaker to the gathered is that of the herald, the "town crier" to the faithful.

You should be able to judge for yourself, among the various plausible forms, which one has the best tuning. One form may not communicate any content whatsoever; another form may lack meaning but have admiration and lyricism about it; still another might be fully comprehensible but lack lyricism. None of them is in proper tune.

Proper tuning can depend on the ability of the priest celebrant; the degree of festivity, the size of the group and the sanctuary— for a gathering of the NPM at a national convetion, a big voice is needed; but it is altogether different when a domestic eucharist is celebrated with eight people around a table.

Tuning also depends on the culture of the listeners. Someone who has never heard a recitative in one's language save at the opera is not necessarily going to enjoy liturgical cantillation. Many forms of expression have disappeared from our modern culture. It so happens that in my village the chief of police used to make proclamations—with drums!

The conclusion is that there is no single good way to do it; even if it's written in the book. In a hymn, for instance, it is the music that carries the bigger portion. The singing of a hymn is very much a community situation, in which the text has less impor- tance than the music.

On the other hand, in all traditions of Christian liturgy there has always been room for those who are able to understand a type of music in which the prayer is centered on the *word* that one speaks, and in which the act of singing consists of giving the word its entire dimension. All Gregorian chant is written in this way: each word finds its dimension.

The idea is that some vocal gestures are much more inter- iorized, in which we "eat" the word. The typical example is psalmody—not sung psalmody, but recited psalmody. The dif- ference is important because in the act of singing, we leave our- selves; with recitation, mandication, we eat the text: it's the oppo- site movement. We are not talking to anyone, for instance, when we recite together the Our Father.

Perhaps at the extreme opposite of this kind of vocal gesture there is the acclamation. Amen, Alleluia, Holy, Hosanna, Kyrie Eleison—are the basis of Christian song. Here participation is the adhesion of all. The relationship is a very strong identification of the entire congregation with the collective gesture. The attitude is the investment of the entire being in the act of singing.

What a great step we'll have made in the liturgy when we no longer hear "Alleluia, alleluia . . ." in a subdued monotone. Rather, one day Christians will be capable of rising up and, in a Paschal night, they will shout: Alleluia! Christ is risen!"

MAKING IT HAPPEN

Mary Alice Piil, C.S.J.

NINE

FOR CONGREGATIONAL SONG, PRAYER IS FIRST

The challenge offered over twenty-five years ago by the participants at the Second Vatican Council continues to face local
churches today: "Mother Church earnestly desires that all the
faithful should be led to that full, conscious, and active participation in liturgical celebrations which is demanded by the very
nature of the liturgy, and to which the Christian people, 'a chosen
race, a royal priesthood, a holy nation, a redeemed people,' have
a right and obligation by reason of their baptism" (Constitution
on the Sacred Liturgy, no. 14).

We've worked to renew our liturgical rites, but have we ac-
complished the goal of active participation? What does it mean
for the members of the local assembly to actually participate in
the eucharistic liturgy each Sunday? Do our assemblies enter into
the reality that is the eucharist? Do they experience the fullness
of the paschal mystery in, with, and through Jesus Christ?

The answer to these questions for most of our membership
today is "No," for the majority of the members in our assemblies
continue to view the offering of the Mass as the act of the priest
alone. In fact, a good number of those gathered to celebrate
eucharist continue to see themselves as passive participants. In
too many instances, as long as a person is singing, dancing, or
making responses, that person is thought to be participating
actively. Not so. A short example might help differentiate between active and passive participation in the liturgy.

A Most Engaging Experience

One of our students, a fine pastoral musician who has been involved in liturgical renewal for years and has come to understand liturgy as the common prayer of the community, attended a funeral liturgy for a Jewish friend. He described the rite as being a most engaging, prayerful experience in which a professional cantor sang the psalms and a rabbi used well-composed, thought-provoking prayers. While the student noted that he neither joined in singing the psalms nor responded to the prayers, he was totally caught up in the liturgy, becoming one of the people praying along with the cantor and rabbi. While externally he did nothing, he was actually engaged in the ritual that enabled him to pray, an active participant in that prayer.

After the rite, the student complimented his Jewish friends on the wonderful liturgy that was theirs. He was surprised by their response. The family did not see themselves as praying; they stated that the rabbi and cantor had prayed for the deceased, and they had simply witnessed the prayer. Most members of our assemblies would no doubt have a similar response if asked about their participation in our common rituals.

To achieve the goal of full, conscious, and active participation, our assemblies must begin to see themselves as active agents of prayer. They must experience themselves as being engaged in common prayer as one body, the church gathered in Christ, their common act of praise addressed to the Holy One through Christ, the head of the body. The prayer of the body of Christ gathered in unity is made under the leadership of the priest-presider.

A Radical Conversion

To begin experiencing oneself as an active agent of prayer demands more than a simple change in the rite. A radical conversion of the believer is essential, a conversion that brings about a totally different understanding of the self at prayer with the gathered community. "We though many are one in him." We, though many individuals, have gathered to pray as one in Christ's name. We, the body of Christ, have gathered to offer the sacrifice of self through, with, and in Christ.

To achieve such a goal, liturgical ministers must appreciate the marriage of liturgy and catechesis. The liturgy itself may be used to catechize a congregation, namely, to bring about a conversion of its members. In that instance we might speak about liturgy *as catechesis*. On the other hand, a congregation can be catechized about the meaning of good worship, and then we speak about catechesis *for liturgy*. This two-fold approach to the relationship between liturgy and catechesis seems an appropriate way to bring a congregation to a new understanding of itself as the active agent of prayer.

Liturgy as catechesis presumes a liturgical celebration that engages all its participants in prayer. Thus the focus is on the task of the liturgy planning committee to make the necessary changes in those liturgical components that are viewed as less than adequately effective at present. For example, the planning team might decide that the communion procession is done poorly and needs work. The way this symbolic gesture will be carried out is discussed in detail at a planning meeting, and whatever changes are deemed necessary are communicated to the assembly in bulletin announcements prior to implementing the changes. Once the procession is in order, then its symbolic meaning can be addressed.

Catechesis for liturgy follows after the community has had sufficient time to make the new approaches their own. At such a time, the homilist is asked to address a particular liturgical experience as part of the homily. Such presentations might be modeled on the homiletic techniques of the early teachers of the church, who used liturgical experiences as starting points for their mystagogical catechesis.

Example: The Responsorial Psalm

Three important moments that are key to greater actual participation in Sunday Mass are the responsorial psalm, the eucharistic prayer, and the communion procession. Each of these elements must be discussed in full by liturgy planning teams to determine their effectiveness in involving the local assembly as participants in the prayer. The responsorial psalm will serve here as an example of both catechesis for liturgy and liturgy as catechesis. Keep in mind that the proposed methodology works from experience to reflection on the experience. But here, to present as succinct an argument as possible, the theological reflection will be presented before the discussion of the experience.

Vatican II called for a radical shift in our understanding of ourselves as the people of God, a people called to enter actively into Christ's mission on earth, proclaiming the message to all. Each member of the faith community is responsible to bring the word of the Lord to their daily life experiences, home, office, school, shop, and so on. It is this experience of our living as members of the Christian assembly that we bring to the Sunday assembly.

The liturgy is to be a true expression of the reality of our living in Christ. Therefore the liturgy of the word is designed to express tangibly, in symbol and gesture, the fact that each member of the assembly is engaged in the ongoing proclamation of the word of the Lord.

We experience Christ present in the word as lectors read and as the priest proclaims the gospel and gives the homily. But we also experience ourselves as proclaimers of the word as we listen to each other sing the responsorial psalm. At this moment the liturgy places the word of the Lord on the lips of all present as we sing the antiphon-response to the psalmist's proclamation of the psalm's verses. We not only listen to the word and are engaged by it, but we also place that word on our own lips, the very word that we have proclaimed in the everydayness of our lives. Here, clearly, the liturgy is not some external ritual that sets us apart from reality, but rather an expression of the very fabric of our being as believers who are alive to the word of the Lord.

In order to assure the possibility of such an experience engaging each member of the assembly in the true reality of the liturgy of the word, each ritual component must be planned with care, particularly the psalm. First, it is to be a psalm, preferably the psalm of the day. The verses are sung by one with the talent to engage the assembly. The assembly for its part sings a response to each verse. (Note that the title "responsorial psalm" does not mean that the psalm is a response to the first reading; the title refers rather to the style of singing—a communal response following each verse. Therefore the practice of choosing a hymn or another reading as "the response to the first reading" is inappropriate.) The responses should be short and easily sung by the average assembly. While the psalm text should be that of the Sunday, the response might be chosen seasonally in order to assure a more dynamic response.

Liturgy planning teams can assist the community's engagement in the psalm by choosing appropriate psalms and responses and by insisting that the psalm with its appropriate response be sung at all Masses. The simplicity of this approach suggests that no prior education of the assembly is necessary in order to implement this change. It is essential, however, that the minister chosen to lead the singing be a person who can engage the assembly in song.

In order to bring about the transformation of the members of our local assemblies into full participants in community prayer, we have to take seriously the challenge of dealing with the liturgy as catechesis and of preparing adequate catechesis for liturgy. There is much work ahead for all of us, but for those committees ready and willing to begin the task, some work with Gilbert Ostdiek's *Catechesis for Liturgy* (Washington: The Pastoral Press, 1986) will be helpful.

TEN

HELPING YOUR CONGREGATION TO PARTICIPATE

If anyone in the history of church music should know about participation, that person must be John Wesley. We can do no better than quote his five principles of congregational singing.

Sing *all*: See that you join with the congregation as frequently as you can. Let not a slight degree of weakness or weariness hinder you. If it be a cross to you, take it up, and you will find it a blessing.

Sing *lustily* and with good courage. Beware of singing as if you were half-dead or half-asleep, but lift up your voice with strength. Be not more afraid of your voice now, nor more ashamed of its being heard that when you sang the songs of Satan.

Sing *modestly*: Do not bawl, so as to be heard above or distinct from the rest of the congregation, so that you may not destroy the harmony: but strive to unite your voices together, so as to make one clear harmonious sound.

Sing *in time*: Whatever tune is sung be sure to keep with it; above all

Sing *spiritually*: Have an eye to God in every word you sing. Aim at pleasing HIM more than yourself, or any other creature. In order to do this, attend strictly to the sense of what you sing, and see that your HEART is not carried away with the sound but offered to God continually; so shall your singing be such as the LORD will approve here, and reward you when HE cometh in the clouds of heaven.[1]

It should go without saying and is evident from the phrase "above all" that Wesley's primary concern is for us to "sing spiritually." For all his dedication to sacred music, it seems that Wesley kept an almost Augustinian reserve about being "carried away with the sound," for musical prayer must first and foremost be prayer.

Platitudinous as this may seem, it is not to be taken for granted. Professional musicians, if they are serious about their work, are naturally concerned with the caliber of their performance. This is clearly the case when significant choral music is performed, but it is only slightly less the case with congregational participation. As pastoral musicians, we want our experience to be as musical as possible, yet musicianship is somewhat easier to measure than true prayerfulness.

Thus, a happy medium must be found between making our liturgical singing a virtuoso concert and allowing it to be half-hearted or lackluster. If we are to pray musically, the music must reach a certain level of quality. We must throw ourselves into the music with the same zest and enthusiasm as a Harnoncourt doing Bach cantatas. At the same time, however, the director must keep in mind that the liturgical aim is the worship of God and not of self. This calls for a special type of asceticism, a determination to keep God in first place.

Vatican II's Constitution on the Sacred Liturgy cautions us that "the sacred liturgy does not exhaust the entire activity of the Church" (no. 9); that "the faithful must come to it with proper dispositions, that their thoughts match their words, and that they cooperate with divine grace" (no. 11); and that "the spiritual life is not confined to the liturgy" (no. 12). It is plain from the New Testament, as well as from the documents of the Second Vatican Council, that any true worship of God must be in "spirit and truth"; otherwise, regardless of solemnity and majesty, liturgy can hardly be called liturgy.

At the same time, liturgy—according to the Constitution on the Liturgy— is "the summit toward which the activity of the Church is directed" and "the fountain from which all her power flows" (no. 10). A liturgy without music is almost unthinkable. Masserman, an ethnomusicologist, points out the importance of music "in helping man to transcend material processes and prosaic fact"—one of liturgy's main functions. A music therapist by the name of Gaston uses music as a tool "to bring about group integration and the establishment of interpersonal relationships." Thus we must view music as an integral part of social worship. Indeed, it is hard to imagine any kind of social gathering without some music, either performed by the group or at least serving as a background or social lubricant.

The socializing, interpersonal function of liturgical music is largely served by congregational participation, and today this is far more taken for granted than it was, say, twenty years ago. While it is possible to listen socially (and this is why concerts remain a deeper human experience than listening to recordings), we have all experienced the difference between merely listening and actually participating. Pope John XXII alluded to this distinction in a talk to a UNESCO group: "Of the means that Providence offers us to purify and elevate ourselves, to escape from selfishness and turn toward universal horizons, music is along the first and highest."

Yet, difficult as any liturgical music is to achieve, all of us who have worked in the field know that it is easier to build up a good choir than a good congregation. There is something about the former that gratifies both directors and performers—perhaps a note of elitism. Further, trained singers respond more easily to direction than congregations. True, there is no substitute for charisma, but this is even less dispensable when it comes to directing a heterogeneous group other than a choir. If a parish is fortunate enough to have a director who can electrify the congregation, hardly anything else is needed.

But what of the less gifted director? In the first place, this person needs the real support of the pastor. The priest celebrant's style can do more to galvanize a parish into participation— whether musical or otherwise—than any amount of cajoling on the part of the director. If the presider truly presides, the problem is half solved.

The choir can be almost as helpful as the priest or the director. First of all, it is obvious (though by no means obvious to everyone) that the space for choir and organ or other accompanying instruments should be up front, visibly related to altar and lectern. The notion of a choir loft toward the back of the congregation, offering a sort of rival musical service, seems too liturgically absurd to need refutation.

The choir can effectively teach and support congregational singing; though its members may not find it especially gratifying, it is surely a true service. For instance, the choir's superior training and reading ability may make repetition a bit boring, for congregations need more repetition than fits the tastes of musicians. On the other hand, the choir can learn descants and other polyphonic accompaniment to the larger simpler sound of the congregation, gradually emancipating the congregation as the new composition becomes familiar.

Rehearsals are inescapable, little as anyone cherishes them. Since congregations cannot be expected to gather other than at liturgical services, congregations can only rehearse before and after these services.

It will make a great deal of difference to the congregation if the director or leader explains precisely what is going on. Why these particular hymns or responses or acclamations? The rehearsal thus becomes clearly related to the liturgy, almost a part of it.

This presupposes that the director, recognized as part of the liturgical team, sits in on planning sessions. It presupposes sensitivity to the needs of this particular congregation, its background, age, tastes, and previous experience. A new director will surely not want to start by eliminating anything, particularly hymns, that the congregation finds enjoyable or at least singable. For one thing, people should not feel needlessly threatened.

It is surprising how dependent people can be on a fixed hymnal or other source of musical materials, such as missalettes. Even people who have only a minimal ability in music reading feel secure in haveing the same, familiar book in hand. It is advisable to adopt one hymnal and stick to it.

There are no panaceas to the problems of congregational participation. But this need not discourage us, as music is itself an aid, not the ultimate purpose of liturgical life. Music can help build up a sense of community, but it can only help if there is something there to build on. While it helps if your choir leader is as dynamic as Leonard Bernstein, even a less gifted person can galvanize a congregation if it is clear that the pastor is in complete sympathy and support; it helps, too, if the conductor radiates assurance and competence. Before a congregation can pray a piece of music, it must possess the music. Confidence, assisted by vigorous accompaniment and direction, can make the difference.

Note

1. As quoted in Rupert Davies, *Methodism* (Pelican, 1963) 114.

Fred Moleck

ELEVEN

CONGREGATIONAL SINGING
WHAT? HOW? WHY? . . . BUT!

It is a rare parish, anymore, that equips its ushers with pistols and instructions to place the gun barrel under the ear lobe of the reluctant singer in the assembly. This technique was sure to elicit a sung response from the believer. There have been other techniques that have been developed over the course of the past two decade. Some are more effective than others. Today, it is equally a rare parish that does not have some type of sung prayer, be it a hymn or an acclamation or a responsorial. The level of the art and craft of the singing and the repertory varies immensely, but the presence of a sung-something is a usual occurence in the American parish.

The journey to get the asesmbly to sing at the liturgy often used devices just as threatening as the cocked pistol—with dubious results. "You will turn to page 14 in the *Parish Prays and Sings* and you *will* sing the entrance song!" Yes SIR. Physical violence may not have always occurred, but the psychic damage is incalculable and injurious to Christian praise.

The journey is still incomplete, but the ground that it covered has been vast, and the tilling has been deep to permit many harvests of sung prayer. If one has traveled along this journey for any length of time, four crucial elements will be familiar. The traveler will undoubtedly have supplemental material, but I hope that the paving of these four areas will be beneficial. Three are most obvious: What do we sing? How do we sing? Why must we sing? The fourth opens old wounds and seeks to heal and encourage: the keystone role of the ordained leadership in liturgical ministry.

WHAT DO WE SING?

Having the temerity typical of an older crusader, I focus on the easiest first: "What do we sing?" There is nothing metaphysical or cosmic in this area. It is the process of trying to find material that the folks in the assembly can sing, that can be learned and assimilated rapdily, and that can cause the assembly to want to sing it again and yet again. It is a search that comes to a close at death—usually the musician's.

This is the area where the musician's tastes are reflective of the limitations and freedoms of his or her own particular history: how the musician was trained, the type of church music valued by the musician, the degree of sophistication in his or her musical taste, and the level of musical competency. These all spiral around the process of choosing music. It is the toe of the spiral that needs to be grounded in the understanding of the place of music in the Roman liturgy from both liturgical and historical viewpoints. When these elements converge, then a sound liturgical judgment can be made in the choice of music. That occurs if the musician is freed by ministerial tempering to choose for the good of the asembly, and this involves a large span of taste and functional choices. The choice will be personal, but it should be relative to, and cognizant of, the elements that make up the process. In all this, vanity has no place.

Herb True, a noted lecturer who resides in South Bend, Indiana, states that the beginning of vanity is the failure to see the greatness in others. He relates that to the dynamics of human encounters, but it also bears much wisdom in the choice of music for the folks to sing. So many battles have been waged over taste-choices by the various camps that line the pews and chairs of the parish church—folk musicians hurling folding chairs at the chorale singers and the chorale singers responding in kind. Energy would be better spent in developing musical styles and items that best serve the *assembly*. A little looking the other way wouldn't hurt either.

The question "What do we sing?" asks for a generic answer—something as inane as: "Something the folks would want to sing again." To sing something again indicates that the experience was a pleasant one, needing to be repeated—hardly the case in much of the musical flotsam and jetsam that now occupies dusty choir file cabinets and organ benches. Much of the early stuff had the appeal of a wet Kleenex and about as much substance. The chant adaptations, the ersatz folk material, and purified versions of some of the Protestant hymns confronted the Roman Church with a repertory that hardly sang of Christian joy and exuberance, but hammered home the style of approved music and texts. These were the collections that were approved for use by the diocesan liturgical and music commissions and were all part of official control and official taste setting. Compared to much of that music, "Kum by ah" looked pretty good, and it was certainly fun to sing.

The folks needed to sing and they needed to enjoy this new experience of opening their mouths at Mass. Too many times the professionals were so cautious that these needs were never met and the folks sought other sources for their new music. Is it any wonder that the music of the St. Louis Jesuits caught afire so fast when compared to the weak-Nelly folk music that was current and the dreadfully dull hymnody that was available? What emerges in stark relief is that the melody was attractive and felt so good to sing. If the melody is expansive, full of good intervallic leaps, and goes up and then down, then it could very well be enjoyed by the assembly in their singing. Puccini and Sondheim are better sources for that type of construct than early Baroque recitatives. The people will sing a good melody. Look at "Eagle's Wings" and "I will raise him/you/them up" and "Gift of Finest Wheat." The melodies are wonderully disjunct, leaping everywhere and violating the rules of what congregational song is supposed to be doing. The effect is one of satisfaction. Satisfaction and appeal are primary considerations in the answering of "What shall we sing?" The item must satisfy and cause the folks to want to sing it again. No matter how correct the counterpoint is or how correct the voice leading is, if the folks don't warm up to it after one or two attempts, it is inappropriate.

The musician's choice is not to re-create yet another Missa Solemnis, but to provide music that the assembly can sing from the heart and with endurance. Such an item is Richard Proulx's "Sanctus" from the Community Mass. It is over twenty years old, enjoys international usage, and satisfies thousands of congregations. The acclamation has endured, proving the tenet that substantial, joyous music that appeals does not mean "fun, fun, fun" and need not reek of Calvinistic constructions.

Certain items demand to be sung again and the assembly seems to be the better for it. It might have been John Calvin preceded by St. Augustine who worried about enjoying sensuality. There is nothing wrong with a sense of well being and comfort joined to a smile when one sings liturgical music.

HOW DO WE SING?

The most defeating part of teaching a congregational item is seeing the assembly's slumped bodies, their tightly drawn lips closed to making utterances resembling the musical pitches, and their look of boredom and dispassionate vision gazing. This area of concern, "How do we sing?" finds its answer in this Sunday morning scenario with a resounding and awesome "With Your Mouths Open!" What should be a requirement for all students in schools of religion, seminaries, and music departments is the faithful watching of Jim Henson's Muppets performing vocal material. There one will see a demonstration of what good vowel projection can be. If Kermit the Frog is beyond the grasp of the members of the assembly, then badger them into the submission of opening their mouths as if they were speaking. There is emerging an entire generation who believe that church singing is orthodontically sealed. Never relent on this practice. "Ah-men" with a big "Ahhh."

Hold Up Your Books. When the books are held at sternum level, the head has to move up into a position where opening the mouth is now possible. It also directs the energy coming from the mouth into the space around the mouth, that is to say, into the space of the assembly where the sound should be. It's a little difficult to hold up a book if the book is flimsy and folds under pressure, but the principle remains the same. When the book is held up, the sound has a fighting chance to get out and be heard. When that happens, some contrast in volume would be possible. All singing does not have to be *fortisimomomo*. Some variations on volume levels can be established once the assembly reaches a plateau of audible sound. This element might take a little time, but the contrast is valuable in enriching the texts.

Make Musical Demands. Once the items are familiar, then re-approach them and do a phrase without an obvious breath mark. Accelerate a given rise in the phrase and show a diminuendo. The assembly should be able to participate in the music ministry by developing some musical sensitivity. Train them. They will respond after they have accepted themselves as public singers—out of their slump and ready to make liturgical song happen.

These two elements can help in the formation of the assembly and their consciousness of who they are. The first assumption is that they are believers at various stages of belief and unbelief who have gathered together for reasons of custom, guilt, conviction, and desire. They are all seeking to make the discovery of the presence of Jesus and to acclaim him for it.

WHY MUST WE SING?

The third element, the *why*, has to do with evangelization and the identity that comes from it. The answer was given by Archbishop Rembert Weakland in 1978 in Scranton when he said that the community would sing if they had reason to sing. Redemption is such a reason. This reason, because of the historical layers that cover it, needs to be reiterated every time the assembly gathers. We must reinforce that we are redeemed; and being redeemed, we should look the part. To be Christian is to be positive and hopeful, and to be Christian in a Roman Catholic liturgy is to accept a thousand-year tradition of human soundings. The music does it the best way. The music creates the most economical bridge into that experience of redemption when it forces us to move from self into communality, the communality that shares the new life. This is reason to sing. That is why we sing. We need to get it out in the open. The process of getting it out in the open is the sharing of the good news. We are thereby thrust into evangelization. The singing, celebrating Christian is the evangelizing Christian. One can never have enough of them.

These three elements of what, how, and why can lead to unflinching optimism and euphoria; that's like having a rehearsal with all parts represented every time, and having the guitarists in tune for every liturgy, and the folks enthusiastically singing every item when it is presented to them. It borders Paradise. And, sometimes, Paradise borders hell.

ROLE OF THE ORDAINED

Despite the commendable efforts of NPM, the extensive continuing educational programs of universities and dioceses, and the growing awareness for constant updating, there are some Neanderthal clergy with whom musicians and the folks are forced to interact. At NPM conventions there are always stories told about this pastor or that associate pastor who refused to attend planning meetings and who bungled the Triduum's rituals. There will be tears shed from frustration when a musician reports how good the music was and how the folks sang their hearts out while the sanctuary presider sent signals of wanting to be anywhere but there with his folks at the time.

Thus the fourth keystone to good congregational song is the visible and invisible, active and passive support of the ordained leadership of the parish. It is not enough for the pastor to sign the check and claim to be supportive of the church's liturgical program. It is not enough to have an appreciation supper for the church's lay ministry. The celebration of the church's life together demands nothing less than the heart, the soul, and the undivided attention of the clergy. Without this element, there is doubt cast on why we must sing as a redeemed people who have something to sing and know how to sing it. That vision of the people of God gathering to give their whole hearts, whole minds, and whole attention to their liturgy is weakened, if not destroyed, by the presider, the deacon, and the lay ministers for that matter, who present the picture of half-commitment and carelessness. Chaucer said it: If the gold rusts, what can we expect of the iron?

When the ordained demonstrate their responsibility as leaders of prayer, when they care so much for their people that they will do everything to assure the best prayer, then the vision gains clarity. Not only will we sound and look like a redeemed people, we will start to act like it; for we shall take great care to assure that our gatherings are profoundly moving and worthy of a redeemed people, both ordained and nonordained, united and visibly committed to our roles of proclaimers and celebrators of the Gospel.

The skills for communicating the gospel mandate lie squarely in the asembly's lap as the gathering is marked with song and prayer. The message of redemption, with all its hope, is loud and clear when the assembly, all its members, are freed to sing by increasing those skills and by the unabashed love and respect the leadership demonstrates to its constituency. The demand of loving those folks is not restricted to the clergy but shared by all of those who have gathered. You gotta love the folks. If you don't, they'll know it.

The Rev. Paul Doyle, former pastor of St. Joseph's in South Bend, is driven to success by the force of his single tenet of administration: "Go in there and love them." True love respects the loved and asks nothing but the best from them, and wants nothing but the best for them. Congregational song is like that— the best from their mouths done in the best manner, because the chosen of God always seek to live with the eternal best.

Frank Brownstead

TWELVE

ON YOUR MARK! GET SET! SING! TEN STEPS

My own experience in observing communities at song and trying to encourage active participation through singing has been varied. Several parishes, parochial schools, a seminary, and a college have been part of that experience. I have no magic formula for lusty, involved, engaged congregational singing—there are too many variables in each situation. But I have observed certain things that seem to pop up again and again. I hope mention of these will be helpful to others.

1. A real community, in the sense that we define a Christian community, *will sing*. In many of our parishes in southern California we are communities only in the sense that we live in the same area and meet in the same building. In some cases our parishes are so large that might better be called cities, and the pastors might better be called mayors. These gatherings are better defined as assemblies. But communities will always sing. Think about a group of high school kids after a week together at summer camp; they will sing. Think about a group of recovering alcoholics celebrating an AA birthday (365 days clean and sober) of one of its members; they will sing. Think about a family gathering for an important event in the life of grandma or grandpa; they will sing. The stronger the bond of love between people in the community, the more natural singing will be.

2. People in an assembly or in a community will sing if there is something to sing about. If nothing is happening, there is really no reason to expect any response from the assembly. If there is no

connection between what is going on in church and the lives of the people, there is little to sing about. People come to church looking for answers about a God they do not understand. People come to church because they are afraid. People come to church because they do things they regret. People come to church because they want to be part of something good that is larger than themselves. People come to church because they are capable of love. People come to church because they want to share their joy. People come to church because they are brimming over with gratitude about a God that does things for them that they could never have done for themselves. People come to church because they want to be more like the God they do not understand. When the singing has something to do with these kinds of reasons for being in church, the people will sing. When the singing has something to do with our lives, it will happen. When the singing just fills in the space, when the singing is distant from our lives, our problems, and our joys, it will be humdrum.

3. The music must fit the liturgy and the people. The bishops' document Music in Catholic Worship talks about the three judgments—musical, liturgical, and pastoral. In this area we are doing much better each year. Musicians and liturgy planners tend to take great pains to see that liturgies are carefully prepared around the readings, with ample input from many people.

Also, more and more parishes are offering many types of musical experiences for parishioners to choose from. Robust singing can be heard even at the Mass at which the choir sings. Choral groups and their leaders see more and more that their real role is to lead and to enhance the sung prayer of the people. That fulfillment of the role of the choir in no way diminishes their importance in the added dimension of beautiful choral work. What distinguish a separate group of people from the rest unless they are offering something really beautiful? Since, today, there is no ritual requirement for a choir, let's not have them unless they fulfill both roles—leadership and beauty.

I single out the choir here because for so long the choir had a different role. Many choirs have accepted their new role painfully and slowly. The good news is that there are more good choirs than ever before. To the extent that choirs and all other singing groups understand their role as musical leaders, our congregational singing can only get better. So, choose the music well, and respect and understand the important roles of the various musical ministries.

4. Cantors and song leaders can help. The leader of song must be trusted by the people. We know that our cantors need skills; not just musical skills and liturgical skills, but also leadership ability. People want to respond to a good cantor; they need to know, with no question, that the cantor is a guide who will always lead them safely through unfamiliar territory. The people have a right to know that their cantor will never leave them "out on a limb." Even when they are sure it is the right time to sing, and know the music well, it is the cantor's invitation that provides that extra bit of assurance and energy. The sensitive cantor can feel what is happening in the community, and will facilitate that existing energy. The cantor encourages life and spirit that is already present. Cantors who get in the way of the natural flow of singing, or who predominate vocally or in any other way, or who have distracting voices, should be eliminated. If singing is to be good, the cantor must be able to be trusted. Some Christian communities have sung without cantors for centuries; if we are going to use cantors, they must fulfill their role.

5. Those who accompany the singing must be competent. Either a person can play the organ or he or she can't. The organist must be capable of playing accurately and with a steady rhythm. If these two components are missing, it is far preferable to try the singing without accompaniment. People simply give up when the accompaniments for the singing defy participation. Of course, for good organists many other refinements can be added to further enhance congregational singing (i.e., interesting registrations, alternate harmonizations, improvising between stanzas, etc.), but it is far better to stick to the two basics—accurate playing and good rhythm—until the people are really able to trust you. Then, go to it, but slowly. Take baby steps. Take a look at *The Organist & Hymn Playing* by Austin Lovelace (AGPDE).

The organists are not the only accompanists who ought to be accountable. Guitarists must all play the same chords at the same time; instrumentalists on the bass line must coordinate their efforts with the other players. Any time these kinds of things are not right, singing will suffer. The singers must be able to trust their accompanists. Remember—accurate playing and impeccable rhythm.

Good organs are essential too. Read *Hymnal Studies Four* by John Fesperman (The Church Hymnal Corporation) for a good description of the role of the organ in our worship, and excellent advice for planning a new instrument. He says: "Liturgical music: liturgical instrument." He also discusses acoustical environment, keeping in mind both spoken word as well as choral and organ music.

6. In parish situations, particularly, coordinate your efforts so that a common repertory will serve many situations. If school Masses, CCD, RCIA, Sunday Masses, confirmation, and first communion are all coordinated so that some common repertory exists, singing will improve. Common acclamations are the starting point: branch out from there. Try preparing a tape of common songs for the year—this saves a lot of time.

7. *Rehearse!* People will sing things that are familiar. If you can find any time for rehearsal with the community, singing will improve faster. When rehearsing, teach just a little bit at a time, with the congregation repeating. Try to find something good about the singing you do hear. Constantly imploring the congregation to sing louder does not always help. Was there something you heard that was worth complimenting? Encourage the people. Why not publicly thank a particular community for their excellent singing when that is appropriate? Keep the rehearsals short and don't necessarily rehearse every week. Find the range that works best for each group. Stress the importance of sung prayer and the reasons for working together to make it better.

8. Build a *repertory* of songs and hymns. Keep track of the things that the congregation will sing well, and gradually add to the list. I tend to discard things that the people won't or can't sing. Perhaps I will try them again later. The major error is to try to learn too many songs. Even if a community learns as few as five or six new songs a year, this is better than romping through dozens of beautifully appropriate hymns with no participation. It is important that the people get the idea that it matters whether they sing or not. Hymns or songs that are not sung are better omitted. Apprehensive communities can often be encouraged to

sing by the use of responsorial forms. This is especially true at communion time, when complicated music falls flat.

9. Some communities can do much more. Try not to hold them back. I have found that the seminary community likes to sing in parts. Because a community that is together every day learns much faster and covers much more territory, their skill at singing will improve faster. Give that kind of community more interesting things to do.

Also, look for variety. Try using rounds. This has been a breakthrough in several situations for me. Have each grade try a verse in the school Mass, if the children are all together. Try alternating boys and girls, or left and right, in antiphonal style. Add bells, instruments, Orff instruments, gestures; the list goes on.

10. Be patient with your community. Try to think of how to be of service to the community. Remember that those of us trained in music will find the people slow and frustrating unless we look beyond music and musical skill to our service role. If we do this, we can be patient, and musical skill will always come as the community grows.

THIRTEEN

HOW CAN WE KEEP
THEM SINGING?

Approximately five hundred people participated in the workshop "How Can We Keep *Them* Singing?" which was presented twice during the National NPM Convention in Long Beach, California, June 1989. The larger group (about four hundred people) came on the first day, and the rest came on the second. Each participant was given a handout titled "Thirty-Eight Bright Ideas on How to Start Building a Strong Foundation for a Singing Congregation" as a way to begin the conversation. The workshop's purpose was presented in this way:

> This workshop is designed to draw out your experience in a way that will help you understand better how to help your congregation to sing and help other parishes evaluate their own situation and encourage congregational singing in their special circumstances.

The process followed had five steps: examine the list of starter suggestions; identify practical and proven ways of getting congregations to sing; group those practical suggestions into major strategy blocks; arrange the suggestions in an ordered way to implement each strategy; and go in peace. The original plan called for participants to divide for strategizing into self-selecting groups, based on the priorities they found in their own situation, but the number of participants made that impossible, so the discussion was conducted by the whole group each day.

The two groups of participants were very different. The larger group entered into the proposed task and process with fairly full

93

cooperation (even though a number of participants reported that the workshop was not what they had expected). The smaller group included people who needed a forum in which to tell their stories, people who were looking for more help than could be given them in this setting. So while the second group was able to complete most of the task set for it, significant time was given over to storytelling and suggestions for individual situations during that session.

Both groups came up with many of the same strategies for getting a congregation to sing, although the second, smaller group developed fewer than the first and larger group. The results of both processes have been combined in this report, with significant differences noted. While the steps described here for each strategy are arranged in order of importance, the six major strategies themselves are not arranged in a particular order. This is because both groups agreed that certain strategies will take priority in some situations, others in different circumstances.

The six strategies concern: repertoire, education, leadership, prayer, physical environment (including instruments), and the surrounding culture. Prayer and the impact of our culture were the least developed categories in the two groups, whereas repertoire suggestions were the most developed.

Repertoire

The participants agreed that when it comes to repertoire, familiarity is the key. Their opinions are expressed in this statement: Repertoire should be built on standard service music and familiar hymnody.

The place to begin is with service music. Each parish should have one or more standard sets of service music that people can rely on. The sets might vary with the seasons, but there should not be too many sets. Likewise, there should be a standard set of familiar, singable, reliable hymns in the repertoire. And each parish should have a standard worship aid (hymnal, missalette, or other form of participation aid) as a basic resource.

The familiar set of standards should be shared among the various music leadership groups, so the same music may be used at all Masses, and so that the congregation will have a reliable set of service music to use when the various music groups combine at special celebrations. This standard repertoire, the smaller group noted, should always be set in a singable range for the congregation. (Note: There was divided feeling in the smaller group over whether different Masses should have a different "feel"—for example, the early morning Mass vs. the choir Mass— or whether the same repertoire should pretty much for used for all the Masses on any given weekend.)

Other suggestions either dealt with particular aspects of the standard repertoire or specified ways to develop familiarity with the repertoire. For instance, there was a strong feeling that congregations should use seasonal psalms, rather than changing the responsorial psalm each week.

It was proposed by the larger group that the standard music should also be used outside worship, in visits to other groups in the parish (for example, to various parish committees and organizations or to retirement communities or health care facilities) or even in a "shopping mall" music ministry. The smaller group proposed that the standard music be used in school and non-school religious education programs, so that the parish's children will be able to sing out at liturgy, and they can become a resource to teach this music to the adults in the parish. All agreed that participation in the repertoire depends on the participation of the clergy, so the clergy should sing their parts that lead into the people's service music.

The way the standard repertoire is used as well as the way new pieces are introduced are further steps in implementing this strategy. For instance, the larger group proposed this general rule: Pick up the tempo and lower the pitch of the music. Any new repertoire should be rehearsed with the congregation (weekly or occasionally) for two to two-and-a-half minutes before Mass. New repertoire should be introduced slowly, used perhaps at first as an instrumental or vocal prelude. And only when absolutely needed should a parish add to its basic resource with a music supplement.

Education

Any educational effort has two "heads," for the leadership needs to be educated about the community's needs if they are to respond in a fitting way, while the community needs formation in and information about the various elements of sung worship. So the agreed educational strategy can be summarized in this way: Each parish should have an educational effort that moves in two directions—from the congregation to the leadership, and from the leadership to the congregation.

There are several ways the leaders can be educated. The liturgy/music leadership should visit and listen to various groups and organizations in the parish. They should also survey the parish to find out its needs and desires for pastoral music (as well as the rest of worship's shape) and meet with a representative group of parishioners for the same purpose.

Even while listening, the leadership should develop an educational effort to train and inform the parish about the role of liturgical music, using music planning and the bulletin to talk about the place of music in parish life and about why we sing. The second group of participants re-emphasized the fact that children can be used to train the adults.

There is a further educational process that should be continuing. The liturgy/music leadership should always be deepening its own education in and understanding of liturgy. For instance, in terms of developing further musical resources, it would be good to consult with experts from outside the parish: the diocese, the cathedral church, publishers.

Leadership

The issue of leadership appeared in concert with all the other strategies, and usually along the following lines: "But if the leaders don't do it . . . or like it . . . it won't happen." So that hard fact, applied to the music leadership, led to this strategy statement: Each parish should have adequate music leadership, people who exercise this ministry through personal presence.

This workshop was initially designed for members of the DMMD (the full-time Directors of Music Ministries Division of the NPM), so it is not surprising that the first step proposed for implementing this strategy came from the larger group this way: Hire a Director of Music Ministry.

In general, however, implementation of the leadership strategy dealt more with matters of presence. Whoever exercises music ministry, the groups agreed, should do so as a whole person, not merely in a "task-oriented" role. Personal presence, attitude, and example are all important. For example, the priest as a leader of sung prayer should be visibly present and rehearsing during rehearsals before liturgy, but such personal presence should infuse all the music ministerial roles. This should be part of the expectation for choirs and cantors, as well as for priests and deacons. As an aid to a more willing personal involvement, the roles of various music ministers at eucharist should be clarified (especially those just listed). All music ministers should be clear about their primary role: to lead, encourage, and support the song of the assembly. The movement of ministers through the assembly—even an occasional seating of the choir in the assembly—can be a physical sign of this central role.

True leadership often arises from a group, rather than being imposed from outside, so it is important to recruit skilled music ministers from inside the parish, to discover and use the gifts of the people, and to challenge people to use their gifts by offering them appropriate music. Finally, since all leadership requires preparation, music leaders should rehearse alone and with others, especially with the assembly.

Prayer

Perhaps it is a measure of our struggle to develop a clear sense of liturgical or ministerial spirituality or to understand how prayer fits into our tasks, but while the participants agreed that prayer is important, they had no practical suggestions on how to implement their general strategy statement: Pray together, especially the leadership.

Environment

The workshop participants had a few more suggestions about practical ways to use the environment to encourage congregational participation, although the strategy was left fairly vague and hopeful: Do what you can to have the physical environment support the congregation's song.

What matters most in our churches these days is the congregation's ability to hear its cues and to hear itself as a singing and praying whole. Other voices and sounds serve the worship-act of the whole congregation. So while older buildings may once have been designed as settings for organs or choirs, or as a kind of tabernacle from which the voice of God (in the person of the preacher) emanated over the heads of the assembled masses, that can no longer be the case. It is important in any building, new or old, to make sure that the space and instruments are used in such a way that the congregation can hear themselves singing. Do what you can to improve acoustics. Do what you can to rearrange congregational seating so that people can support themselves vocally and visually. Have a decent sound system and instrument (organ), with the organ preferably up front. Know how to use both of these properly. If necessary and useful, put the whole music ministry up front.

Culture

As with prayer, the participants knew that the culture in which we live and move and have our being is important and has a significant impact on congregational participation, but they had no specifics to offer as ways to implement this final strategy. This strategy was mentioned by the second, smaller group, who were determined that we should avoid various "bashings," such as "clergy-bashing," "congregation-bashing," and "musician-bashing." They felt the same way about culture. We have all heard how our present musical culture makes it difficult for people to sing in church, but we need to find out what positive support that culture can offer. Hence this final statement: Use whatever the surrounding culture can offer to support sung prayer.

THE MUSICIAN

FOURTEEN

TEN COMMANDMENTS FOR THOSE WHO LOVE THE SOUND OF A SINGING CONGREGATION

Parish music directors come in a great variety of shapes, sizes, and styles. When we compare one with another, we usually think in terms of their musical competence: do they know how to choose good music, and can they perform it well? But even the best church musicians can be further divided into two different groups or categories.

For example, let us consider "the case of John and Mary." Both are very talented musicians who direct music programs in two parishes on opposite sides of the same city. John is very devoted to the great works of the sacred choral and organ literature. He finds his chief motiviation in the preparation and performance of these works and tries to use them during the liturgy as often as possible. Mary follows a more eclectic course in planning the music. She tries to achieve a balance between the best of the old and the best of the new. (John would probably say that her tastes are too "secular.")

John has little time to devote to the improvement of the congregational singing or for working with the "less interesting" musical parts of the liturgy. He believes that most of the members of the congregation want to be left alone and would rather listen to the organ and the choir. Eventually, the appreciation for good sacred music may "trickle down" to them, and then perhaps they will be motivated to sing. The congregational singing in Mary's church would be rated "fair, but steadily improving." She tries to provide the assembly with strong leadership, both visibly and audibly, and places a priority on the singing of the acclamations and responses. It has been a struggle, but her choir members are finally beginning to realize the importance of their role as members of the assembly and leaders of its song. Now at their rehearsals, they always make sure they know the hymns and responses before practicing their anthems.

John's pastor respects him for the fine musician he is, and for the most part he lets John "do his own thing." They have brief meetings before Christmas and Easter, but usually their communication is limited to checking last minute signals on the intercom between the sacristy and the choir loft. Mary is a member of her parish liturgy committee. She is also considered part of the parish staff and meets regularly with her pastor to assess the progress of the music program.

Both John and Mary are church musicians, but only one of them is truly a pastoral musician. Of course, good pastoral musicians must, first of all, be good musicians. Some of the music they perform can and should include the sacred music of our Christian tradition. But this is only part of the total picture.

In our renewed understanding of music as an integral part of worship, the dimension between sacred and secular music is in many ways no longer valid. As Aidan Kavanagh has written: "Liturgical music is neither 'sacred' nor 'secular'; it is liturgical; that is, liturgical music is any music that serves the assembled faith community and its values in ritual engagement."[1] If the distinction continues to have any validity, it does not pose the question: Is this music sacred or is it secular? The important question is rather: How is this music used by the discerning pastoral musician? Thus it really has to do more with *persons* than with *things*.

"Secular" musicians have their own set of values that include the striving for excellence in performance and the appreciation of good music. "Sacred" (pastoral) musicians must add to these values a sensitivity to the demands of good liturgy. "Secular" musicians may be motivated in the performance of their art by a variety of reasons. "Sacred" (pastoral) musicians must be motivated *primarily* by the desire to *serve* the praying assembly *through* the art of music.

Good pastoral musicians first of all claim their musical art by perfecting their musical knowledge and skills. The following "ten commandments" for pastoral musicians suggest some ways they can then proceed to claim their *special* art.

I

Pastoral musicians must learn to love the sound of a singing congregation above any other musical sound. Some may consider this an exaggeration, but I believe it is absolutely crucial. In a very real sense, the primary musical instrument of the pastoral musician is not the organ or the piano or the guitar but the singing of the assembly itself. Many times we become so involved in developing a good choral or instrumental sound that we forget that the musical prayer of the assembly is our primary concern. To be sure, it is not usually a polished sound; rather, it is rough-edged and slightly out-of-tune. But if it is also a strong and authentic sound, it provides a measure for successful liturgical music more accurately than any other voice or instrument.

II

Pastoral musicians must be concerned about the spiritual health of the communities they serve. This is the other side of the coin. If the assembly's singing is weak, the problem may be a liturgical or musical one. But it may also be primarily an ecclesial problem. If the bonds that join the members of the community are very weak, if its members do not have some sense of belonging to and being responsible for each other, then its singing will also be half-hearted. In this case, the musician should not be expected to shoulder the total burden of improving the participation when the problem is much deeper. On the other hand, the musician should be willing to give help and support to those who are ultimately responsible for seeing that the community bonds can begin to grow stronger.

III

Pastoral musicians must learn to appreciate a variety of musical instruments and styles. Notice that the word is "appreciate," not simply "tolerate." Obviously, musicians have varying personal tastes, and they cannot help but be reflected in the general style of the musical programs for which they are responsible. But those

who completely avoid particular styles or instruments—"traditional" or "contemporary"—are forgetting the nature of their
ministry. Many times, personal tastes must be set aside. Pastoral
musicians have the duty both to encourage their congregations to
be open to many styles of good liturgical music and to be per-
ceptive in discovering the particular styles that best serve the
prayer of their parishes.

IV

*Pastoral musicians must be able to work with a variety of liturgical
song forms.*There are at least six song forms used in the liturgy,
including acclamations, brief responses, litanies, responsorial
songs, hymns, and choir anthems. Whereas an anthem may be
musically more interesting than an acclamation, it is not nearly as
crucial to the liturgical prayer. Musicians must give more attention to these shorter musical forms, working with them imagina-
tively and learning to weave them into the fabric of the liturgical
action. A good music program includes a balance among the
different forms, not relying too heavily on one or the other. It
includes not only solid hymns and choral music, but also responses and acclamations that are strong and spontaneous.

V

*Pastoral musicians must be able to communicate effectively with their
congregations.* A musician who says: "I will sing and play for the
congregation, but please do not ask me to stand up in front to
teach or lead them," cannot be pastorally effective in the long run.
In other musical fields, a person can say: "Here is my music; take
it or leave it." But in the liturgy, strong communication is essential. It is hoped that the music itself is clearly communicated, as
in the case of an organist who knows how to really lead a hymn
with a firm and articulate style of playing. But usually more is
needed. An inviting personal presence, good eye contact and
facial expression, strong gestures, and a clear, positive approach
when giving explanations and introductions: all these elements
are important factors in helping the pastoral musician to be a
good communicator.

VI

Pastoral musicians must be able to work as members of a team. There is no room for the "rugged individualist" or the temperamental artist who gets terribly upset when presented with suggestions or constructive criticism. The exact shape of the "team" responsible for the liturgy varies from parish to parish. In many cases, the music director is an *ex officio* member of the parish liturgy committee. At the very least, there must be good communication and cooperation between the pastor and the musician. This is not to say that a music program should be directed by a committee. Trained musicians must be responsbile for the specific musical planning and performance. But they must also be open to the other members of the team for general planning and direction as well as feedback and evaluation.

VII

Pastoral musicians must have a good knowledge of Scripture. Careful study of the scriptural readings for a particular liturgy is an important step in the process of musical planning. On a deeper level, the Bible has been and continues to be the chief source for the texts of our liturgical songs. The musician who take time to study the word of God is able to better appreciate and perform these songs and to communicate this appreciation to others.

VIII

Pastoral musicians must be people of faith. Of course, this may have nothing to do with the quality of the musical performance itself. A non-believing organist may play considerably better than a believing one. But pastoral musicians who attempt to keep the rest of these "commandments" cannot be effective ministers unless they are fellow travelers somewhere on the road of faith. Eventually, it will be obvious to those they serve not so much by what they do as by how they do it.

IX

Pastoral musicians must be people of prayer. This flows from the previous point, but it adds another dimension. As Music in Catholic Worship states: "Christians' faith in Christ and in each other must be expressed in the signs and symbols of celebration or it will die" (no. 4). As musicians, do we pray in our homes? Do we begin our rehearsals with prayer? Do we pray with the other ministers before the liturgy? And most importantly, can we see through all the technical details of our performance so as to experience the liturgy as our own prayer?

X

Pastoral musicians must be proud of their vocation. On several occasions I have met musicians who seemed to consider their church performance as "second-rate"—not as demanding or fulfilling as teaching or concert performance. This may be true for those who cannot see beyond the music itself. But those who strive for excellence in performing the music and their ministry have a vocation of which they can be proud. They are called not only to use the musical talents with which they have been blessed, but also to be musical instruments of the sacred.

Note

1. Aidan Kavanagh, "Beyond Words and Concepts to the Survival of Mrs. Murphy," *Pastoral Music* 1:4 (April-May 1977) 18.

FIFTEEN

CLAIM YOUR ART

Music cannot really be talked about; it has to be experienced. In the same way, liturgy cannot be described, but must be experienced. Talking can help us understand and judge the experience, but it can never be a substitute for the experience.

The story is told that Schumann, having just finished a composition, invited some friends from Heidelberg University to listen to it. After he had played it through, somebody asked him: "But what does it mean?" His reply: "It means exactly this." And he then played it over again. The simple lesson is that music has to be lived.

If our worshiping people of God are to have frequent good experiences of liturgical music, then it is important that we do not shun those musical and liturgical experiences that stretch our skin a bit. The musical and liturgical experience that will profit us most are those that take us into a new dimension of life.

One Saturday night in Rome I went to a concert conducted by Stockhausen. What generally happens in Rome at a concert of modern music is that, after about the first five minutes, half the people in the audience get up, shake their heads, and, saying there is nothing for them to sing in the bathtub, leave. This happened at the Stockhausen concert. I noticed, however, that those who did stay (not the professional musicians, who seldom like to have their skin stretched, but mostly nonprofessionals who were curious, if not fascinated) talked much during the intermission. They were understanding, appreciating, and enjoying the music. Their skin had been stretched, and they placed no obstacles to the experience.

The experience of liturgy and liturgical music cannot be totally measured by an emotional yardstick. Music in liturgy does not have to be at all times a peak experience in order to be valid musically and liturgically. Liturgy is always a symbolic act; therefore we bring to that act all our life experiences, all our religious experiences, wherever and whenever they may take place. Each liturgical experience does not have to be total, or we would all go insane with satiety. Liturgy and liturgical music must evoke and make real all our previous experiences, liturgical and just plain religious, we have had in life.

For example, I cite two of the great moments of my own existence. The first was seeing Mount Sinai. I went there shortly after the Six-Days War. We had driven through the night in jeeps and arrived in the morning: before us was that mass of rock. To me this was a great religious experience. I said to my companion: "God could speak here." I remember also the first time I entered Santa Sophia in Istanbul; I didn't want to talk to anybody. These are experiences, religious experiences, that liturgy simply evokes in us again and brings back; they are moments of God's presence, God's power in our lives. Although I wish to emphasize the importance of the experiential, I do not want to create the impression that your task, each time, each Sunday, is to create Mount Sinai or to create Santa Sophia. It simply means that all the experiences that people have had, and they have many, have to somehow find themselves re-evoked in the liturgy.

We—the people of God—need something to make music about.

Every time you hear the music of certain composers of liturgical music, you sense, hear, that there is something being given us to sing about, to make music about. This is the foundation of pastoral music. The faith dimension of our lives seeks an outlet in art, in music. Without it, we end up with only an esthetic experience. It is not that the esthetic experience is wrong; but do we then make that quantum leap in faith so that the esthetic experience can bring us closer to the Lord?

St. Paul, when he wrote to the church at Colossae, said: "The peace that Christ gives is to be the judge in your hearts, for to this peace God has called you together in one body. And be thankful. Christ's message, in all its richness, must live in our hearts. Teach and instruct one another with all wisdom. Sing psalms, hymns, and sacred songs. Sing to God with thanksgiving in your hearts" (3:15-17). This is where pastoral music comes from: from a deep faith committment, something to make music about.

Once when I was traveling in Africa, I had left Abidjan on the Ivory Coast early in the morning to fly to Togo. We had just taken off when one of the jet's engines was totally in flames. You can be sure that I prayed my breviary very devoutly at that time. The fuel was jettisoned and we made a forced landing. To get to Togo I finally had to fly to Nigeria and backtrack on an old BC-3. Finally at 6:00 that evening, I reached my destination. A group of about thirty women, all Benedictine oblates, had waited all day at the airport for me. Letitia was the president of the group; it reminded me so much of the early church. As you may know, the society of Togo is matriarchal, and the women are large, buxom, and very maternal. Although I was tired and nervous from the flight, once Letitia gave me that big embrace and a kiss of peace I began to revive again.

We all gathered in her home where two things happened that have remained very vivdly imprinted on my mind. First of all, while we were eating supper, there was a very, very elderly woman sitting in the corner singing. She sang through the whole meal. The ladies told me that she knew the entire psalter by heart and would improvise melodies for it as she prayed. At the moment when I asked they told me she was singing Psalm 119—the longest in the psalter. They kept telling me that it all came from her heart and was indeed her prayer.

When the supper had ended, I made a short speech. In the middle of the speech I said something that seemed to trigger an important reaction on the part of all the ladies. Suddenly they jumped up and started to sing and clap their hands and formed a circle and paraded around the room as they sang. At first I did not know why, but then Letitia explained to me that it was what I had said. "It's so great, so beautiful, so important to us, we had to sing." All I could say was: "Thanks." Although it broke the continuity of my text, it did not matter, because suddenly they had something to sing about; and when you have something to sing about, then you must sing and dance and parade around the room.

We have all been in situations of deep tension and a certain sense of oppression or helplessness. In such a moment we all know what it is like to sing. "We shall overcome." It suddenly brings everyone together, lifts one's spirits, and gives a sense of hope and courage. Perhaps you are familiar with the account of the young lad in Chile who was taken prisoner at the end of the Allende regime. He was held with others in the stadium. During this waiting period he began to play his guitar and everyone began to sing. The guards, of course, were disturbed by such unity. Soon his guitar was taken from him and smashed. He was taken out of the stadium, and returned with his fingers cut off. After a short while, however, everyone began to hum and sing again just as he had. This time the guards took him out and when he returned, all could notice the blood coming from his mouth, as his tongue had been cut out. When he began to sway in the rhythm of the song, all caught on and began to sing again. This time he could be stopped only with a bullet. There is something about music that makes even a totally heterogeneous group suddenly come together as a unity. This happens because they have something to sing about.

God's people need something to sing about.

It is not enough just to make music, but it is God's people who have to be making music and singing. They are the ones who count. We call it pastoral music because it is theirs. To avoid the strange connotations of the term "folk" music, I prefer to call it people's art or people's music. It must be a communal expression and a communal experience of faith and belief that finds its expression in music. In this sense, people's music has no place for eccentricity or idiosyncrasy. It must be a product that everyone can claim as being true to who they are. Everyone has to "own" it; it is shared art, it is art—work—that everyone feels and senses in their being. For such kind of music to exist, that is, people's music, there has to be a tradition and a culture. There is a need for keeping a culture alive. It is amazing how fresh sometimes one or the other of those old Latin songs can be when we hear them anew.

In 1968 I went to Bangkok, Thailand, for a meeting between Buddhist and Benedictine monks. It was the first meeting of this sort, and organizing it had not been easy; people were certainly not comfortable with the idea. The western monks did not know how to dialogue with eastern monks, and many of the superiors from western nations who had come to be present were a bit frightened by the need for adaptation and acculturation of monasticism. The meetings started off in a very shaky fashion. Thomas Merton was one of the principal highlights of the event and delivered his famous speech on Marxism and monasticism. At that time most of us present did not understand the urgency of the theme. In fact, many felt a bit surprised that he had not spoken on the relationship between eastern and western contemplation. The liturgies had all been prepared ahead of time, but were the "least-common-denominator" kind that would offend nobody, but that culturally also belonged to nobody.

Merton died during that meeting. As I was anointing his warm body, I could sense already a change in all the participants. The group began to pray together and really in depth. They went into small groups and were constantly at prayer. At that point language did not matter, nor did discussion. And suddenly, the group seemed to come together. The next morning I presided at the funeral liturgy; the alleluias of the resurrection were sung with such feeling that I will never forget the experience. We decided to continue as Merton would have wished, and it turned out then to be an excellent meaning. I hope he somehow realizes how he had contributed to making that meeting become a true sharing and not just a series of monologues.

God's people need something to make music about when they worship together.

Pastoral music also has a liturgical dimension. We should never forget that this dimension is an integral part of our *métier*. We must be sensitive indeed to liturgy, to where people are in their lives. I wonder if our sermons would not be much better if we would begin not by meditating on Scripture, but by reflecting on where people are when they come to church on Sunday morning. One could say perhaps the same thing to the liturgical musician: what kind of people are coming to church this Sunday morning, what problems are they bringing with them, what do they want to take home with them to be able to face a real world? If we begin this way, then we are indeed sure what we are ministering to and our reflections can be applied from the Gospel more easily.

One thing is absolutely clear: the text and the words that are spoken in the liturgy, and the entire experience itself have to say something to real people. If we want to sing ten verses of the hymn, fine; but each verse must truly be important and have content. We have gained sensitivity to word since Vatican II, and we cannot simply say things or make music without it making sense to definite people. For these reasons you should be much more cautious about your texts. If we have learned anything from the new liturgy, it is that every text is important. From the moment a person arrives to worship in church until that person leaves, every aspect of the event, and especially the text, is important and must be given consideration. In this way we feed our people, nourish them, as pastoral musicians should, and give them something not just to sing about *then*, but something to sing about in the whole of life.

Let me tell another story. This time I am in Upper Volta, in its capital Ouagadougou. We have a little monastery called Zubri, about twenty miles outside the city. Without doubt, it is the poorest area I have ever visited. It lies in the savanna, where there is really nothing, literally nothing. I would get up early in the morning just to look out of my window to watch the women, from grandma down to the smallest child, with big calabashes on their heads, walking eight miles to the nearest well to bring the water back before the sun got too hot. This is poverty. But one of the greatest experiences of my life happened there on Sunday morning. Everybody came from the valley up to the monastery—monasteries are always on hills—and there we had a very simple liturgy, simple instruments, simple songs. I didn't understand the dialect, but I celebrated the Mass and preached in French. After I finished my sermon, I thought the catechist was going to translate it, but he started to sing. The prior of the monastery told me that he had put the theme of my sermon into an antiphon for them, a refrain; and they all sang it back. He sang—literally— my entire sermon, point by point. And as he sang, they put in the refrain consistently to the end. During the communion I heard the same melody again. At the end of Mass they all went forth singing the theme of my sermon. Then they sat under the trees, where the brothers instructed them. I heard them going back into the valley that night singing the refrain. Here is indeed an example of something pastoral, in which people have something to take home, something to sing about.

In this context I want to underline something that Matthew Fox once said, namely, that in liturgy there has to be not just word to take home, but *commitment*. Liturgy is then something that transforms not only the people present, but everybody out there as well. It is something that can change society.

God's people need something to make music about when they worship, and that music must be art.

It is difficult not to think immediately in terms of elitism. It is unfortunate that today we make distinctions like classical and pop or commercial music, serious music versus light music, and so on. Previously there was a distinction between church and secular music, but it could all be classified as artistically good. Why is art important in church music? Why has the church through all these centuries held on to art? Art always implies the correct dosage of emotion and intellect; nothing runs wild in art. It cannot be excessive or uncontrolled. Whether it be a simple little tune or a tremendously complicated piece of music, it is always disciplined and controlled. This is why the church has always used art.

Stravinsky was the great proponent of this idea in our own day and has much to say about the need for discipline and control, if music is going to be true art. Toscanini spoke often about the same; he always had under his control all the emotion he needed plus one degree more. He would never let it run away with him. True art is always controlled and disciplined and gives the right dosage at the right time. If it isn't so, then it is saccharin—too much sugar; or it is insipid—too much salt. The right dosage requires an enormous amount of discipline and control. This is why you must yourselves be disciplined, controlled people, if you want to truly be artists and help our own people to produce this right dosage. I am never afraid of a great composer becoming frenetic. Even when Stravinsky was writing the Rite of Spring, the most frenetic music of all, he produced controlled freneticism. This kind of discipline, discipline of emotion, is a part of art.

The important thing for us is first to acquire this discipline and, second, to see how each dosage must be given in the liturgy at the right time. You can have the right bottle on the shelf, but put it in the wrong soup. And just because a piece of music is ready does not mean it can be served; it has to fit the proper moment.

God's people need something to make music about when they worship, and since this music must be art, professional artists-musicians must serve God's people with their talents.

This is a pretty logical conclusion, isn't it, to what has come before? And without any doubt, those people have to be you, you who are pastoral musicians.

When I graduated from Juilliard in 1954, the commencement speaker was William Schumann, the composer and president of Juilliard. I usually do not remember commencement addresses (especially those that I have to give), but at that commencement, in sum, he said: "Everybody out here, all of you, will have to find out who you really are as pianists. Only one or two of you will really make it big; the rest will have to be content to be church musicians." Bach and Mozart would have blushed to have heard those words. Consider yourselves as the logical successors of Bach and Mozart. The difference is that today you must always be a team minister; you must always be working with others to create the musical liturgical experience. Your calling is not just a profession; it is truly a *calling* and *being sent* by God. The more people in the church see themselves as called and sent to do a mission, namely, the work that Jesus gave us, then, of course, the more Christian we will all be.

The mission is not just to create a nice experience within the church walls; we have to go out also and take it to everyone. Choirs should always go outside the church, to the nursing homes, to the sick; get out there, see what life is about. Consider yourselves as sent, and make sure that the melodies that come out of that deep faith also reach the marketplace. Once they reach the marketplace, then there will be truly new songs, because the marketplace has its own cares that will also bring their ferment to the song itself.

God's people need something to make music about when they worship; and since this music must be art, professional artists-musicians must serve God's people with their talents, and those people must be you. God is calling! Claim your art by accepting God's call.